The Old Burying Ground
at Sag Harbor
Long Island, New York

Compiled by
Dorothy Ingersoll Zaykowski
and
*Members of the Committee for the
Old Burying Ground*

HERITAGE BOOKS
2006

HERITAGE BOOKS

AN IMPRINT OF HERITAGE BOOKS, INC.

Books, CDs, and more—Worldwide

For our listing of thousands of titles see our website
at
www.HeritageBooks.com

Published 2006 by
HERITAGE BOOKS, INC.
Publishing Division
65 East Main Street
Westminster, Maryland 21157-5026

International Standard Book Number: 978-0-7884-2347-9

Table of Contents

Photographs

INTRODUCTION

In 1997 a small group of concerned citizens in Sag Harbor, Long Island, New York, met to discuss what could be done about the deteriorating condition of its ancient and historic burying ground. Time, weather and vandalism had taken their toll, and help was long overdue. A committee formed, and work soon began to improve this important part of the village's heritage.

Throughout the years, stones had been broken, moved, and overturned. A thorough inventory of the grounds had not been done since Louis Tooker Vail did his over a half a century ago. The fence was in a bad state of disrepair, and litter had found its way amidst the remains of Sag Harbor's founding fathers.

The committee's first project was to do a new inventory and record, measure, and photograph each stone. Of the 335 gravestones located, there were some that had never before been recorded. Over twenty-five stones had somehow found their way to a pile under a cedar tree at the crest of the hill. These stones were returned to their correct locations and re-set in the ground. The committee then divided the burying ground into ten grids and numbered each stone. A display case was built and installed near the entrance of the cemetery which holds a map of the site, showing each stone and instructions on how to go about finding a particular burial site.

The Peconic Monument Works were hired to re-set many toppled stones, and some of the broken ones have been restored. Lichen and moss have been removed, and cleaning has revealed names, dates and epitaphs that had been unreadable for decades.

The old cast iron fence that encloses two sides of the burying ground has been scraped, primed and painted where possible. Several sections cannot be saved and will have to be replaced.

Slide shows, lectures and tours for both adults and children have been presented to better inform the public of the importance of preserving this resting place of Sag Harbor's early citizens. And finally, through the efforts of the committee, ownership of the Old Burying Ground has been transferred from Southampton Town back to the Village of Sag Harbor.

We have accomplished much, but there is always more to do. Upkeep is never-ending, and the committee welcomes any interested resident to join us in this vital job of preserving our Old Burying Ground for future generations.

The Committee for the Old Burying Ground

**The Committee for the Old Burying Ground
at Sag Harbor, L.I., N.Y.**

Contributors to the Book

Barbara Cronenberger, Andrea Meyer, Susan Rowland, Paul Saurer, Barbara
Schwartz, Dorothy Sherry, Dorothy Ingersoll Zaykowski
Photography by Stephen Peters

Past and Present Members

Stephen Barr, Ruth Birkhoff, Emily Bodenheimer, Barbara Cronenberger, Richard
Cullen, Suzan Smyth Habib, Shirley Kessel, Robert Lewis, Robert McDade, Molly
McDonald, Andrea Meyer, Elisa Nevel, Stephen Peters, Joseph Ricker, Susan
Rowland, Paul Saurer, Barbara Schwartz, Dorothy Sherry, Frances Stafford, Lois
Beachy Underhill, Lillian Vishno, Dorothy Ingersoll Zaykowski, Dolores
Zebrowski.

A BRIEF HISTORY OF THE OLD BURYING GROUND

The first mention of opening a burying ground in what was then the growing port of Sag Harbor is found in the Southampton Town Records, when in May 1767, the Trustees of the Town voted and ordered that, "William Rogers and David Woodruff shall purchase a piece of land at Sag Harbor near the Meeting House, not to exceed 3/4 of one acre, to be for a burying place and that at the Town's cost." Up until that time, a small cemetery apparently stood on the northwest corner of Church and Sage Streets, as early burials were unearthed while digging a foundation there.

The September 1, 1859 issue of the *Sag Harbor Express* told of a meeting held in the Village Hall regarding the burying ground. At that meeting, William Fordham, an aged citizen of Sag Harbor, stated that his mother told him the Town had acquired the land from David Hand and that it was called "Burying Yard Hill." The property stood a block south of the Meeting House and was bounded by Union Street to the north, Madison Street to the west, and Latham Street to the south.

Tradition tells us that the burying ground was used soon after the property was acquired and that Sag Harbor's Tory innkeeper, James Howell buried his two infant sons there in 1767. It was positively in use by 1770, or six years before the American Revolution, for at the 1859 village meeting, Eleazer Latham stated that he had in his possession, deeds dating 1770 and 1772. These deeds described a piece of nearby land as being, "bounded west by the burying ground. In those early times, before stone walls on the east and west side of the burying ground were constructed, the place was enclosed by a picket fence. Much of the property south of Union Street was still woodland, for the "settled" part of the Port at that time went no further, and land had to be cleared as the cemetery increased in size.

During the Revolutionary War a British fort stood at the crest of Burying Yard Hill and was described as being, "crowned with a breastwork and ditch, and the space within armed." It is believed by some that the outline of this Revolutionary ditch is still visible along the Madison Street side of the cemetery. When plans were formulated to build the Presbyterian Church on Union Street in 1843-44, several of the local parishoners were incensed when they learned the church was to be built on land so close to, and possibly over the site of some of the earliest burials. One individual voiced his opinion loudly and clearly in an 1843 letter to the Sag Harbor *Corrector*, in which he angrily stated that if they tampered with the remains of his loved ones, he would do them bodily harm. Nevertheless, over the objections of some, the church was built and a stone wall constructed between it and the burying ground.

Throughout the seventy-three years of its use, the burying ground became the resting place of a myriad of people: early settlers, wives and children, whaling captains, Revolutionary War Patriots, African American residents and Portuguese seamen. Then, in 1840, with plots at a premium, Oakland Cemetery and St. David AME Zion Cemetery opened, and within a few years, the Old Burying Ground fell into a state of neglect and disrepair.

In 1859 a group of concerned residents of Sag Harbor held a meeting and a committee was formed to investigate the cost for making necessary improvements and repairs in the Old Burying Ground. They reported that the place was in a deplorable condition and "herds of cattle and troops of unruly boys roamed its grounds, desecrating the ashes of the dead." The stone wall on the Madison Street side was rapidly deteriorating and they were afraid that with the Spring rains, it might collapse and take with it the remains of those buried along the west side. The front row of burials were only two feet from the wall, and in 1860 a decision was made to remove at least fifty and take them to Oakland Cemetery for re-burial. Before the job was over and the wall removed in 1863, the remains of one hundred and thirty-nine individuals were moved.

Suggestions were made by those attending the village meeting as to the best way to preserve the Old Burying Ground. William Gleason felt the entire ground should be leveled with the Presbyterian Church yard, walks laid, grass planted, and a common grave of all those interred be placed in the center with a monument over them.

Another thought that after the wall was removed they should build a terrace and have a gate on the Madison Street side opposite Jefferson Street, with steps leading up into the cemetery. Enoch Eldredge, who favored preserving the burying ground as it stood, felt the answer should be an iron fence, and that it would be well worth the $1000 cost. However, none of those ideas were followed through at that time, and another picket fence was built around the cemetery. It remained standing for the next seven years until Sag Harbor's newly formed Village Improvement Society had the existing iron fence installed in 1887.

Found in the Old Burying Ground are a variety of stones: limestone, marble, slate, sandstone and schist: many embellished with wonderful carvings of cherubs, urns, soul effigies, weeping willows and portraits. The stones not native to this area were imported from New Jersey and Connecticut, and some carved by Ithuel Hill, a stonecutter who came to Sag Harbor from Connecticut in 1793 and started a business here.

In 1885 William Wallace Tooker, a local druggist and archaeologist, inventoried the stones in the Old Burying Ground, some which at that time were already 100 years old. His findings were published in the East Hampton Town Records, Volume V. In 1950 a second inventory was completed by Louis Tooker Vail. Since then over fifty years have passed, and the weather, lichen, and vandalism have taken their toll. Broken and toppled stones are abundant and many stones are now extremely difficult to read.

In 1997 a Committee for the Old Burying Ground was formed, made up of concerned citizens interested in preserving and caring for this important part of Sag Harbor's history. We have done the most extensive and thorough inventory ever undertaken in the Old Burying Ground, recording information on the 334 stones, copying over 150 epitaphs, scraping, painting and restoring much of the 113 year old iron fence. Each stone has been numbered and the cemetery divided into ten grids, making it easier to locate burial places.

In 1999 an archaeological dig was conducted in the Old Burying Ground by Tracker Archaeology Services of North Babylon, with the hopes of discovering artifacts from the fort that stood there. Although some traces of 18th and 19th century habitation was suggested, no significant data was unearthed from the test holes that were dug at random locations throughout the burying ground.

There is still much to do. Re-setting toppled stones, repairing broken stones, cleaning stones and removing lichen, and planting a ground cover on the slope along the Madison Street side to prevent further erosion, are all future projects. One might think that stone is something that can't be easily damaged, but as Dr. Gaynell Stone, noted authority on colonial gravestones said, "stones are living things, far more fragile than we assume. They freeze, they thaw, they exfoliate, they get eaten by lichens." We, the members of the Old Burying Ground Committee feel it's pretty amazing that after two and a quarter centuries, so many still survive.

References : **A Brief History of the Old Burying Ground**
Trustee Records of the Town of Southampton, NY (Part I) 1741-1826.
Sleight, Harry D., 1931.
Sleight, Harry D., *Sag Harbor in Earlier Days*. Bridgehampton, NY :
The Hampton Press, 1930.
Zaykowski, Dorothy Ingersoll, *Sag Harbor: the Story of an American
Beauty*. Mattituck, NY : Amereon Press, 1991.
The Sag Harbor Express: assorted articles from 1859.
The Sag Harbor Corrector: 1843 letter.
OBG Inventory of William Wallace Tooker, 1885.
OBG Inventory of Louis Tooker Vail, 1950.
Tracker Archaeology Services, North Babylon, NY, 1999.

D. Zaykowski

HELPFUL HINTS
"Cleaning Stones"

The process of slowing down the deterioration of gravestones
in your burying ground can be achieved by keeping the stones clean
and free of lichen.

Ancient graveyards fall prey to a number of adversities over the
years. Although you have no control over the elements which does its
share, you can help keep the stones in a healthier condition by
removing all harmful growth on them. Mold and lichen, with their
many colors and types, invade ancient stones and cause them to
deteriorate rapidly. Cracks widen and layers flake off when lichen is
allowed to grow and weaken parts of the surface.

Using a popsicle or craft stick, or a bristle brush, most lichen
can be safely removed. Never use a metal tool, knife or wire brush.
To clean further, a solution of one part amonia to four parts water,
brushed on the surface will help, as long as it is flushed off with plenty
of clear water.

Evaluate the condition of the stone, and if damage is too
severe, it is best not to clean it without professional guidance.

ALPHABETICAL INDEX OF BURIALS IN THE OLD BURYING GROUND WITH GRAVESTONE NUMBERS

47 Baker, Nathaniel; Peirson, John
51 Bates, David
145 Beckwith, Captain Richard
72 Beebe, Alletta
76 Beebe, Bethiah
73 Beebe, Jason
69 Beebe, Lester
76a Beebe, Captain Lester
71 Beebe, Nancy
70 Beebe, Captain Thomas
131 Bird, Mary E.
46 Blank, Anne
238 Boardman, Frances
304 Bridges, George Washington
54 Brown, Captain David
53 Brown, Jemima

197 Chase, John
17 Clark, Aaron
12 Clark, Captain Aaron
20 Clark, Anne
15 Clark, Huldah
16 Clark, Huldah (base)
64 Clark, Rebecca
27 Coleman, Shubal
77 Coles, Mary Ann
312 Collins, Elizabeth
187 Collins, Jane
309 Collins, Rebecca
310 Collins, Luther Halsey
313 Collins, Samuel
137 Condlon, John S. (footstone)
228 Conklin, Jonathan
134 Conklin, Mary (footstone)
263 Cook, Albert
261 Cook, dau. of Henry & Zeruiah
139 Cook, Charles Henry

262 Cook, Mehitabel
207 Cook, Nehemiah B.
277 Cooper, Henry
321 Corey, Abraham
322 Corey, Abraham, Jr.
236 Corey, Braddock
237 Corey, Charity
189 Corey, John B.
230 Corey, Phebe
188 Cory, Charity
25 Corniell, Timothy
33 Crowell, Marcy
3 Crowell, Sally

123 Dalosta, Juan Antonio
333 Davis, Sylvester
173 Dennison, Nancy
63 Douglas, Catharine
62 Douglas, Mary Ann
175 Duvall, Mary
176 Duvall, Mary
317 Edwards, Albert
318 Edwards, Elihu
319 Edwards, Elizabeth
55 Edwards, Phebe K.
320 Edwards, Samuel
102 Eldredge, James
100 Eldredge, Lucy
186 Eldredge, Mary
37 Eldredge, Mary G.
85 Eldredge, Sally
82 Eldredge, Sarah
101 Eldredge, William

243 Fordham, Abigail (base)
235 Fordham, Betsey
269 Fordham, Charles

257 Hildreth, Christiana
79 Hildreth, Eliza Ann
256 Hildreth, Henry
258 Hildreth, Captain John
225 Hildreth, Luther Brown
221 Hildreth, Captain Luther
219 Hildreth, Mary
220 Hildreth, Mehitabel
218 Hildreth, infant of Luther
52 Hill, John Price
229 Hobart, Sarah
223 Horton, Hainulal
267 Howell, Benjamin
268 Howell, James Boyle
266 Howell, Sylvanus

125 Ignaios, Esther
18 Ives, Emeline

115 Jack, Judith
30 Jagger, Abigail
32 Jagger, Benjamin
31 Jagger, William
91 Jessup, Louise
92 Jessup, Stephen
86 Jones, Hannah
278 Jones, Mary C

316 Kendrick, Mary
142 Knaps, William M.

126 Labanja, Francisco
59 Latham, Almy (possibly)
60 Latham, Eleazar
57 Latham, Emmeline
56 Latham, Mary
65 Leek, William Mulford
303 Lesliuce, John Sherman
44 L'Hommedieu, Capt. Ephraim
45 L'Hommedieu, Mehitable

43 L'Hommedieu, Joseph
272 L'Hommedieu, infant
of Charles
128 Lucianni, Francisco
119 Lugar, Cynthia B.
50 Lugar, Eunice

88 Matthews, Ann Elizabeth
90 Matthews, Betsey
89 Matthews, Charles
87 Matthews, Harriet
116 Miller. Brewster
325 Mitchell, John Carrol
323 Mitchell, Virginia
334 Mott, Nathaniel

21 Niles, Ephraim
22 Niles, George
23 Niles, Peleg
24 Niles, Phebe
281 Norton, Sophia
282 Norton, Captain Thomas

133 Oakley, Samuel
245 Overton, Jemima & child
215 Overton, Charles E.
214 Overton, John H.

127 Panna, Joachim Joze
248 Parker, Hannah
165 Parker, Captain Henry
240 Parker, Hettie
252 Parker, Captain James
249 Parker, James H.
66 Parker, John W.
67 Parker, Joseph
299 Parker, Mary Abigail
302 Parker, Nancy
164 Parker, Nancy Maria
68 Parker, Phebe

190 Stuart, Austin	291 Wade, Charles R.
273 Stuart, Roxana	287 Wade, Jared
193 Stuart, Silas	290 Wade, Lucetta Augusta
	292 Wade, infant of Jared
78 Tarbell, David	1 Wattles, Juliette
212 Taylor, Amy	29 Welden, Susannah
210 Taylor, Nancy	227 Whittlesey, Eliza Tully
213 Taylor, William	147 Wiggins, James
42 Topping, Jerusha	146 Wiggins, Mical C.
	111 Wood, Priscilla
38 Truman, Clark	112 Wood, Robert
117 Tucker, Tamos	270 Woodward, Caleb
	271 Woodward, Mary
288 Wade, Catharine	
289 Wade, Charles G.	41 Youngs, Mary

The following individuals are listed in the Louis Tooker Vail Inventory, but their headstones are no longer standing. Some of the broken bases and fragments listed below undoubtedly belong to them.

Lester Beebe, Jr., son of Captain Lester & Bethiah Beebe, who died July 13, 1796, age 19.

_____ Baker (probably the wife of Nathaniel J. Baker).

Jerremiah Gardiner, died May 1, 1825, age 32.

Sir John Oldmixon, died December 6, 1817, age 56.

Albert Rogers, died July 31, 1833, age 2 1/2.

Sarah Russell, wife of David Russell, died June 22, 1816, age 68.

Nathan Stuart, (church records his death October 14, 1816). age 38.

Roxana Fordham Stuart, daughter of Nathan & Roxana, died December 1805.

John S. Condlon (possibly Conklin), died June 25, 1837, footstone remains.

Infant Daughter of Henry & Mary A. Conklin, died November 3, 1846, footstone remains.

11 illegible stone (unknown)
26 footstone "JH" (possibly John Price Hill)
36 broken base (unknown)

39   fragments (unknown)
40   broken base (unknown)
84   broken base (unknown)
103 _____ Charles E.
110 _____ Clarissa W.
113 broken base (unknown)
124 broken base (unknown)
132 fragments (unknown)
180a footstone "TRH" (possibly a Harris)
194 footstone (unknown)
209 footstone "NH"
251 broken base (unknown)
275 footstone (unknown)
276 footstone "HF"
301 footstone "NP" (possibly Nancy Parker)
306 footstone (unknown)

Nathaniel Baker and John Peirson, stone # 47
Baker and Pierson lost their lives celebrating the return of peace between the
United States and Great Britain, at the end of the War of 1812.

OLD BURYING GROUND NUMBERED STONES

The names below are all of the burials marked with stones, their number, and in which grid they can be found. The letters indicate if the entry has a headstone (H), footstone (F), epitaph (E), support stone (S), and if they were listed in early inventories done by Louis Tooker Vail (V), William Wallace Tooker (T), unlisted in either (UN), and Revolutionary War Patriots (*).

GRID #1

1	H	**Wattles, Juliet**, wife of Dr. Wm. Wattles, 10/12/1841, age 30.	V
2	HE	**Hatfield, William**, son of Smith & Catherine 9/12/1843, age 18.	VT
		Hatfield, John, son of Smith & Catherine 9/12/1843, age 16.	VT
3	HFE	**Crowell, Sally**, wife of Asa 10/10/1806, age 26.	VT
4	HF	**Hedges, Jeremiah**, 6/12/1832.	V
5	HE	**Hedges, Mary**, wife of Jeremiah 9/1/1839, age 70.	V
6	H	**Hedges, Betsey B.**, dau. of Jeremiah & Mary 2/17/1818, age 19.	V
7*	HF	**Squire, John**, 6/2/1807, age 68.	VT
8	H	**Squire, Hannah**, wife of John 6/5/1811, age 68.	VT
9	HF	**Rogers, Mary**, 7/13/1796, infant.	UN
10	HF	**Raymond, Elizabeth**, dau of William & Thankful, 11/25/1790, infant.	VT
11	H	Illegible	
12*	H	**Clark, Capt. Aaron**, 6/11/1855, age 98.	VT
13*	HFE	**Price, Benjamin**, 12/8/1818, age 79.	VT
14	HF	**Price, Mary** (base) wife of Benjamin 6/10/1817, age 68.	V
15	HF	**Clark, Huldah**, dau of Aaron & Huldah 9/12/1813, age 15.	V

16	H	Clark, Huldah, (base), wife of Capt. Aaron 1/26/1837, age 70.	VT
17	HF	Clark, Aaron, son of Aaron & Huldah 10/5/1800, age 2.	VT
18	HE	Ives, Emeline, wife of E.R. Ives 5/10/1832, age 28.	VT
19	HE	Roberts, Sally, 11/30/1796, age 10.	V
20	HF	Clark, Anne, wife of Aaron 9/11/1821, age 90.	V
21	HFE	Niles, Ephraim, son of Peleg & Phebe 10/23/1804, age 17.	V
22	HFE	Niles, George, 10/7/1823, age 32.	VT
23*	HF	Niles, Peleg, 9/27/1828, age 63.	VT
24	H	Niles, Phebe, widow of Peleg 5/11/1829, age 62.	V
25	HFE	Corniell, Timothy, son of Stephen & Prigtel 12/1/1801, age 2.	V
26	F	footstone (JH) possibly John Price Hill #52	V
27	HF	Coleman, Shubal, son of Benjamin & Ruth 7/3/1789, age 18.	V
28	HE	Smith, Egbert, son of Stephen & Catherine	UN
29	HE	Welden, Susannah, dau of Jonathan & Mehitabel, 3/16/1792, infant.	VT
30	HFE	Jagger, Abigail, relict of Capt. William 3/4/1795, age 43.	VT
31	HF	Jagger, William, son of William & Abigail 10/28/1788, age 8.	VT
32	HE	Jagger, Benjamin, son of William & Abigail 9/15/1788, age 1.	VT

GRID # 2

33	H	Crowell, Marcy, wife of Stephen (also infant) 12/5/1793, age 44.	VT
34	HFE	Godbee, Mary Ann, dau. of John & Lydia	

		8/17/1817, age 21.	VT
35	H	**Godbee, Evelena**, dau. of John & Lydia	
		4/4/1802, age 1	VT
36	HE	broken base	unknown
37	H	**Eldredge, Mary G.**, dau. of Enoch &	
		Evealina, 4/29/1836, age 1.	VT
38*	H	**Truman, Clark**, 10/2/1795, age 59.	T
39	HF	fragments	unknown
40	H	broken base	unknown
41	HE	**Youngs, Mary**, dau of David & Mary	
		11/10/1836, age 12.	T
42	HF	**Topping, Jerusha**, wife of Luther	
		2/18/1820, age 24.	V
		(moved to grid #3 before Jason Beebe # 73)	
43*	HF	**L'Hommedieu, Joseph**, 5/9/1788, age 69.	VT
44*	HF	**L'Hommedieu, Capt. Ephraim**, 5/30/1795,	
		age 40.	VT
45	HFE	**L'Hommedieu, Mehitable**, wife of Ephraim	
		10/19/1815, age 65.	VT
46	HF	**Blank, Anne**, wife of Ephraim	
		3/22/1826, age 27.	V
47	HFE	**Peirson, John & Baker, Nathaniel**, 2/25/1815	
		both age 22.	VT
48	HF	**Price, Isaac**, 9/21/1808, age 33.	VT
49	HF	**Price, Capt. John**, 8/14/1809, age 40.	VT
50	HF	**Lugar, Eunice**, wife of Christopher	
		9/30/1841, age 64.	VT
51	HE	**Bates, David**, son of Capt. Isachar & Hannah	
		9/13/1789, age 20.	V
52	H	**Hill, John Price**, son of Rufus & Patience	
		9/30/1793, infant.	V
53	HE	**Brown, Jemima**, wife & infant of Capt. David	
		8/4/1821, age 38.	VT
54	HFE	**Brown, Capt. David**, 3/21/1835, age 54.	VT
55	HFE	**Edwards, Phebe K.**, wife of Silas W.	
		11/25/1836, age 48.	V
56	HFE	**Latham, Mary**, wife of Daniel	
		1/28/1811, age 29.	VT

57	HFE	Latham, Emmeline, dau of Daniel & Mary 0/12/1801, infant.	V
58	HFE	Spooner, Alden, son of Alden & Rebecca 11/28/1809, age 2.	VT
59	HF	broken headstone and footstone "AL" (possibly Almy Latham, dau of Eden Shotwell and Martha, 10/3/1803, infant.	V
60	HF	Latham, Eleazar, son of Capt. Peleg & Matsey, 8/20/1785, age 21.	T
61	H	Spooner, Deborah, widow of Juda 3/28/1823, age 70.	T
62	H	Douglas, Mary Ann, dau of Charles & Catharine, 9/13/1817, age 21.	V
63	HF	Douglas, Catharine, wife of Charles 3/1/1825, age 52.	V
64	HFE	Clark, Rebecca, wife of Capt. Moses 10/21/1809, age 39.	V
65	HE	Leek, William Mulford, son of Jacob & Harriet, 10/12/1819, infant.	UN

GRID #3

66	H	Parker, John W., 12/6/1832, age 37.	VT
67	H	Parker, Joseph, 4/7/1835, age 73.	VT
68	HF	Parker, Phebe, 7/31/1836, age 66.	VT
69	HFS	Beebe, Lester, son of Capt. Thomas & Nancy, 11/18/1834, age 36.	VT
70	HFS	Beebe, Capt. Thomas, 8/21/1822, age 58.	VT
71	HF	Beebe, Nancy, wife of Capt. Thomas 2/20/1832, age 67.	VT
72	HF	Beebe, Alletta, wife of Jason 9/2/1838, age 45.	VT
42	HF	Topping, Jerusha, wife of Luther 2/18/1820, age 24. (moved from grid 3 to put with her footstone)	V
73	HFE	Beebe, Jason, son of Capt. Lester & Bethiah 9/4/1835, age 48.	VT

74	HE	Fordham, Edgar Fowler, son of Frederick & Samantha, 1/2/1832, age 1.	V
75	HE	Fordham, George Frederick, son of Frederick & Samantha, 1/13/1832, age 3.	VT
76	HF	Beebe, Bethiah, wife of Capt. Lester 2/17/1823, age 63.	V
76a*	H	Beebe, Capt. Lester, 11/11/1832.	V
77	HE	Coles, Mary Ann, dau of Thaddeus & Phebe, 9/23/1820, age 1.	T
78*	HF	Tarbell, David, 12/24/1833, age 88.	T
79	HF	Hildreth, Eliza Ann, dau of Capt. John & Phebe, 3/30/1822.	T
80	HFE	Fordham, Hugh G., 5/19/1835, age 33.	VT
81	HF	Fordham, Latham (headstone & base). 4/4/1827, age 37.	V
82	HE	Eldredge, Sarah, 9/20/1821.	UN
83	HF	Gawley, Mary Eliza, dau of Joseph & Sabrina 7/9/1822, age 1.	V
84	HF	broken base unknown	
85	HFE	Eldredge, Sally, wife of Stillman 3/9/1817, age 32.	V
86	HF	Jones, Hannah, wife of Ezekiel 6/18/1810, age 27.	V

GRID # 4

87	H	Matthews, Harriet, dau. of Nathan & Betsey	UN
88	H	Matthews, Ann Elizabeth, dau of Nathan & Betsey, 1/22/1833, age 1.	V
89	HE	Matthews, Charles H., son of Nathan & Betsey 1/19/1811, age 8.	V
90	HE	Matthews, Betsey, wife of Nathaniel (Nathan) 1/19/1848, age 37.	VT
91	HF	Jessup, Louise, wife of Stephen 8/13/1830, age 71.	VT
92*	HF	Jessup, Stephen, 11/28/1833, age 75.	VT
93	HF	Hall, Jonathan, son of Rev. Daniel Hall	

		8/12/1837, age 61.	VT
94	HF	**Hall, Mary**, dau of Rev. Daniel Hall	
		2/10/1831, age 45.	VT
95	H	**Fordham, Harriet**, dau of John & Emma	
		2/5/1824, age 1.	V
96	H	**Gardiner, Ann Maria**, dau of Stephen H.	
		& Ann E., 5/6/1827, age 1.	V
97	H	**Halsey, Edward Warren**, son of Capt.	
		Jesse & Mary, 6/26/1836, infant.	V
98	HE	**Smith, Capt. Elkanah**, 12/1/1826, age 39	V
99	H	**Smith, Elkanah**, 10/13/1838, age 21.	VT
100	HFE	**Eldredge, Lucy**, wife of William	
		1/12/1820, age 52.	V
101	HF	**Eldredge, William**, 2/16/1837, age 73.	VT
102	H	**Eldredge, James**, son of Sylvanus & Sarah	
		8/27/1817, age 10.	VT
103	H	_____, Charles E. (broken headstone)	UN
104	HF	**Smith, Charles Lewis**, son of Capt. Charles	
		& Ruth, 2/1/1818, age 1.	T
105	HF	**Smith, Sarah Ann**, dau of Capt. Charles &	
		Ruth, 9/11/1820, infant.	T
106	HFE	**Smith, Ruth B.**, wife of Capt. Charles Jr.	
		8/18/1826, age 32.	UN
107	HE	**Fordham, Theodore Bertrand**, son of	
		George & Frances, 9/12/1843.	T
108	HE	**Fordham, Clarissa Dering**, dau of George	
		& Frances, 3/20/1838, age 8.	V
109	H	**Fordham, Clarissa Frances**, dau of George	
		& Catherine Frances, 2/21/1821, age 1.	VT
110	H	_____ **Clarissa W.**, dau of John &	
		Catherine, 3/3/1836.	UN
111	HFE	**Wood, Priscilla**, wife of Stephen D.	
		2/6/1813, age 25.	V
112	H	**Wood, Robert H.**, son of Stephen & Priscilla	
		8/31/1813, age 1.	V
113	H	broken base unknown	
334	H	**Mott, Nathaniel**, son of Elisha, 4/22/1825,	
		age 1.	UN

(this stone was found buried behind a hedge
in the burying ground and was the last numbered.
We decided to leave it near the spot it was found
in Grid 4).

GRID # 5

114 H	Rogers, Hiram, 11/17/1811, age 10.	VT
115 H	Jack, Judith, (African American) 4/7/1828, age 75.	V
116 HE	Miller, Brewster, (African American) 1/28/1846, age 75.	V
117 HE	Tucker, Tamos, (African American) 12/13/1799, age 66.	V
118 HE	Smith, Abigail, dau of Elias & Charlotte 6/13/1843, age 1.	V
119 HE	Lugar, Cynthia B., wife of George, 10/8/1834, age 18.	VT
120 H	Gibbs, Daniel, 2/28/1834, age 71.	V
121 H	Robin or Robert, (African American) 3/16/1798, age 24.	V
122 HFE	Prince, Caroline, (African American) wife of Simeon, 3/12/1830, age 41.	V
123 HE	Dalosta, Juan Antonio, son of Antonio & Maria Luiza, 5/28/1845, age 20. (Portuguese sailor) V
124 H	broken base unknown
125 H	Ignaios, Esther, dau of Francisco Ignaios and Jennet M. DeMilo, 4/20/1845, infant. (Portuguese) UN
126 HE	Labanja, Francisco, 10/12/1843, age 21. (Portuguese sailor)	V
127 HE	Panna, Joachim Joze, 7/17/__, age 21. (Portuguese Sailor)	UN
128 E	Lucianni, Francisco, 6/18/__ . (Portuguese sailor)	UN
129 HE	Francisco, Manuel, 7/24/1833. (Portuguese sailor)	UN
130 HFE	Snook, Charles, 7/2/1854, age 34.	UN
131 HF	Bird, Mary, (African American), dau of John &	18

		Rachel, 2/7/1841, age 11.	V
132		fragments unknown	
133	HE	**Oakley, Samuel,** 1/16/1841, age 34.	VT
134	F	footstone "MC" possibly **Mary Conklin**	
		8/6/1772, age 12.	V
135	HS	**Solomon, Elizabeth,** (African American) dau	
		of Samuel & Mehitabel, 12/21/1819, age 15. V	
136	HE	**Solomon, Mehetabel,** (African American)	
		wife of Samuel, 6/25/1828, age 46.	V
137	F	footstone "JSC" **Condlon, John S.**	
		6/25/1837, age 23.	V
138	H	**Fordham, Clarissa,** wife of Thaddeus	
		5/9/1824, age 51.	V
139	H	**Cook, Charles Henry,** son of John & Hannah	
		7/20/1832, infant.	V
140	HFE	**Russell, Lynus,** son of John & Sarah	
		9/7/1832, age 1.	V
141	HFE	**Scovil, Percey,** 8/7/1836, age 70.	V
142	H	**Knaps, William,** son of William & Sally	
		9/16/1833, infant.	V
143	HE	**Halsey, Mariah,** dau of Henry & _____.	UN
144	HFE	**Smith, Phebe Ann,** dau of Daniel & Phebe	
		10/6 /1827, age 2.	UN
145	HFE	**Beckwith, Capt. Richard P.,** 7/23/1832,	
		age 32.	V
146	HFE	**Wiggins, Mical C.,** 7/30/1838, age 36.	V
147	HFE	**Wiggins, James,** 10/27/1829, age 61.	UN
148	HFE	**Smith, Capt. Lewis,** 11/22/1828, age 55.	UN
149	HFE	**Smith, Lettis,** wife of Capt. Lewis	
		8/3/1841, age 72.	UN
150	HFE	**Smith, Obid,** 1/14/1834, age 63.	V
151	HFE	**Smith, Mercey,** wife of Obid	
		3/25/1836, age 54.	V
152	HE	**Sherman, Elizabeth D.,** widow of Baldwin	
		9/26/1857, age 45.	V
153	H	**Sherman, Henry C.,** son of Baldwin &	
		Elizabeth, 1/9/1847, age 2.	V

Grid # 6

154	HFE	**Havens, John Nicoll**, son of Silas & Proculah 10/6/1798, infant.	V
155	HFE	**Havens, Cordela**, dua of Silas & Proculah 9/1/1799, infant.	V
156	HFE	**Havens, Proculah**, dau of Silas & Proculah 2/6/1796, infant.	V
157	HE	**Gardiner, Hannah**, wife of Jeremiah 5/4/1820, age 37.	T
158	HFE	**Smith, Henry L.**, 7/21/1843, age 24.	V
159	HE	**Smith, Elizabeth**, wife of Joseph 10/20/1823, age 28.	V
160	H	**Smith, Silas Hand**, son of Joseph & Elizabeth 9/13/1826.	V
161	HFE	**Smith, Capt. Joseph**, 8/2/1831, age 34.	V
162	HFE	**Foster, Hannah**, wife of Peter 9/25/1803, age 48.	V
163*	HFE	**Parker, Capt. William**, 10/2/1832, age 78.	V
164	HFE	**Parker, Nancy Maria**, dau of William & Phebe, 10/12/1828, age 22.	V
165	HFE	**Parker, Capt. Henry**, son of Capt. William & Asenath, 10/31/1840, age 63.	V
166	HF	**Furman, Maria**, wife of William.	UN
167	HFE	**Sayre, Capt. Silas** and his son (**Isaac Wickham**) 4/13/1811, age 44.	V
168	HE	**Sayre, Wickham**, 11/10/1806, age 27.	V
169	HFE	**Sayre, Jeremiah**, 6/17/1804, age 23.	V
169	HFE	**Sayre, David, Jr.**, 12/19/1800, age 23.	V
170	H	**Sayre, David**, son of Nathan & Priscilla 10/7/1801, infant.	V
171	HF	**Sayre, Alanson**, son of Nathan & Priscilla 10/13/1800, age 1.	V
172	H	**Sayre, Alanson**, son of Nathan & Priscilla 8/16/1805, age 1.	V
173	HF	**Dennison, Nancy**, dau of Samuel & Phebe 6/6/1796, age 1.	V
174	H	**Sayre, Nathan & Priscilla**, Nathan	

10/7/1826, age 52. Priscilla, 10/8/1832, age 57.

175 H   **Duvall, Mary,** dau of William Jr. & Mary
9/5/1791, age 7.   VT

176 HF   **Duvall, Mary,** wife of William Jr.
8/31/1795, age 44.   T

177 HF   **Satterly, John,** son of Capt. Stephen &
Margaret, 11/10/1810, age 12.   V

177a HE   **Satterly, Andrew,** son of Capt. Stephen &
Margaret, 9/29/1791, age 12.   V

178 HFE   **Satterly, Margaret,** wife of Capt. Stephen
11/11/1805, age 47.   VT

179 HFE   **Harris, Thomas L.**
1/19/1831, age 68.(with Henry D.)   VT

179 HFE   **Harris, Henry D.,** 11/27/1823, age 25.   VT

180 HFE   **Harris, Amma (Amy),** wife of Thomas L.
8/10/1829, age 67.   VT

180a F   footstone "TRH"   (possibly a Harris)
(this stone has letters on reverse side)

181 HE   **Harris, Lucretia S.,** dau of Thomas & Amy
4/2/1814, age 17.   V

182 HE   **Harris, Sarah Scott,** dau of Thomas & Amy
8/14/1803, age 13.   VT

183 HFE   **Harris, Keturah,** dau of Thomas & Amy
6/13/1794, age 6.   VT

184 HF   **Hand, Hannah,** wife of Josiah
1/9/1799, age 34.   V

185*HFE   **Hand, Josiah,** 12/12/1835, age 79.   VT

186 HF   **Eldredge, Mary,** wife of James
7/6/1809, age 26.   VT

187 HF   **Collins, Jane,** wife of Samuel
7/12/1818, age 33.   VT

188 HE   **Cory, Charity,** dau of John & Phebe
9/30/1799, age 5.   VT

189 HF   **Corey, John B.,** 12/7/1813, age 52.   VT

190 HFE   **Stuart, Austin,** 9/3/1798, age 28.   V
(next to Austin Stuart is a square fieldstone
possibly marking an unidentified burial)

191 HFE   **Pierson, Lucretia,** wife of Hervey

		6/11/1830, age 41.	VT
192	HFE	Stuart, Abigail, wife of Silas Sr.	
		7/16/1816, age 76.	VT
193*	HF	Stuart, Silas, 11/16/1800, age 57.	V
194	F	footstone unknown	
195	HE	Stewart, Polly, wife of Silas Jr.	
		3/17/1801, age 23.	VT
196	HF	Stewart, Silas Jr., 12/1/1839, age 61.	V
197	HFE	Chase, John, 3/5/1796, age 29.	V
198*	H	Havens, Capt. William, 1/1/1797, age 51.	V
199	H	Fordham, Thomas, son of Samuel &	
		Jemima, 8/25/1798, infant.	V
200*	HF	Fordham, Frederic, son of Capt. Daniel &	
		Phebe, 6/25/1782, age 18.	V
201	HFE	Fordham, Samuel, son of Samuel & Jemima	
		2/27/1803, age 32.	VT
202	HF	Fordham, Phebe, wife of Capt. Daniel	
		11/4/1806, age 70.	VT
203*	HF	Fordham, Capt. Daniel, 6/12/1816, age 86.	VT

Grid # 7

204	H	Peirson, Edward, son of Hervey & Nancy,	
		12/16/1807, infant.	V
205	HE	Sherard, David (native of Ireland)	
		8/24/1810, age 31.	VT
206	HFE	Goodwin, John, Jr., 6/10/1784, age 43.	VT
207	HFE	Cook, Nehemiah B. (portrait stone)	
		3/4/1792, age 25.	VT
208	HFE	Hall, William Lester, 8/4/1803, age 28.	VT
209	F	footstone "NH"	
210	HF	Taylor, Nancy, wife of William	
		9/20/1803, age 26.	VT
211	HFE	Hard, Nabby (Abigail) wife of Lemuel	
		2/13/1804, age 24.	V
212	H	Taylor, Amy, wife of William	
		6/22/1832, age 47.	VT

213	HF	Taylor, William, 12/23/1846, age 76.	VT
214	H	Overton, John Hick, son of James & Elizabeth 9/27/1809, infant.	V
215	H	Overton, Charles E., son of Francis D. & Betsey, 8/8/1836, infant.	T
216	HFE	Halsey, Sally, wife of Job 11/29/1801, age 42.	V
217	HE	Halsey, Nancy (see #209- possibly Nancy's footstone) 10/29/1836, age 16.	T
218	H	Hildreth, infant son of Luther & Abigail 3/6/1793, infant.	V
219	H	Hildreth, Mary, dau of Capt. Luther & Mehitabel, 6/3/1789, age 1.	V
220	HFE	Hildreth, Mehitabel, wife of Capt. Luther 7/31/1791, age 32.	VT
221*	HE	Hildreth, Capt. Luther, 12/11/1826, age 71.	V
222	HFE	Hildreth, Abigail, wife of Capt. Luther 4/20/1836, age 73.	T
223	HFE	Horton, Hainulal ,wife of Capt. J.Havens Horton, 2/16/1809, age 28.	V
224	HFE	Sleight, Henry Augustus, son of Henry & Cornelia, 9/23/1829, age 1.	T
225	HE	Hildreth, Luther Brown, son of Samuel & Phebe, 9/18/1826, age 1.	T
226*	HF	Hedges, Dr. Jeremiah, 8/17/1797, age 51.	V
227	HFE	Whittlesey, Eliza Tully, dau of John & Sally, 8/8/1805, age 1.	VT
228	HF	Conklin, Jonathan, 3/8/1803, age 74.	V
229	HFE	Hobart, Sarah, wife of Benjamin K. 1/9/1803, age 30.	V
230	H	Corey, Phebe, wife of John B., 8/19/1818 age 59.	VT
231	HFE	Foster, Rebekah, dau of Thomas & Rebekah, 8/24/1793, age 23.	V
232	HE	Foster, Joseph W. Jr., 10/28/1868 age 73.	V
233	H	Foster, Joseph W., 1/5/1843, age 78.	V
234	HF	Foster, Sarah, wife of Joseph W.	

		11/23/1859, age 89.	V
235	HFE	Fordham, Betsey, wife of John	
		9/11/1796, age 28.	V
236*	HF	Corey, Braddock, 2/1/1809, age 74.	VT
237	HFE	Corey, Charity, wife of Braddock	
		2/12/1775, age 33.	VT
238	HFE	Boardman, Frances, wife of Daniel	
		12/20/1824, age 60.	T
239	HFE	Ripley, Lydia, wife of Capt. Joseph	
		9/5/1795, AGE 59.	VT

Grid # 8

240	HFE	Parker, Hettie, dau of James & Hannah	
		4/26/1870, age 64.	V
241	HFE	Hand, Sally, wife of Capt. Isaac	
		3/18/1792, age 21.	V
242	HF	Havens, Captain Daniel, 5/25/1789, age 40.	V
243	HFES	broken base/stone Fordham, Abigail wife of	
		Nathan, 9/15/1796, age 62.	V
244*	HF	broken base Fordham, Nathan, 11/13/1805	
		age 83, and Fordham, Sarah, 11/12/1805	
		age 70.	V
245	HF	Overton, Jemima, wife of James	
		12/16/1807, age 29.	
		and daughter, 2/10/1807, infant.	V
246	HF	Hathaway, Catharine, wife of Gilbert	
		11/26/1816, age 30.	V
247	H	footstone (no initials) unknown	
248	HE	Parker, Hannah, wife of Capt. James	
		8/17/1824, age 42.	UN
249	HE	Parker, James H., son of Capt. James	
		& Hannah , 3/25/1849, age 35.	V
		(in front of #249 is a sandstone base)	
250	HFE	Higbie, Maria Sleight, wife of Aaron H.	
		4/11/1832, age 24.	V
251	H	broken base unknown	

252 HF	Parker, Capt. James, 6/28/1848, age 71.	V
253 H	Parker, Rebecca, widow of Capt. James 9/16/1849, age 49.	V
254 HF	Parker, Sarah, dau of Capt. James & Rebecca, 5/1/1865, age 34.	V
255 HF	Sandstone base and footstone unknown	
256 HFE	Hildreth, Henry, son of Capt. John & Christiana, 8/29/1815, age 20.	V
257 HF	Hildreth, Christiana, wife of Capt. John 9/8/1805, age 37.	V
258 HE	Hildreth, Capt. John, 10/27/1805, age 42.	V
259*HE	Gelston, Hugh, 4/26/1828, age 73.	VT
260 HFE	Gelston, Puah, wife of Hugh 8/27/1829, age 68.	VT
261 H	Cook, _____ dau of Henry & Zeruiah 11/26/1803, infant.	V
262 H	Cook, Mehitabel, dau of Henry & Zeruiah 9/24/1805, infant.	V
263 H	Cook, Albert, son of Henry & Zeruiah 12/23/1806, infant.	V
264 HE	Gelston, Elizabeth, widow of David 3/23/1858, age 77.	V
265 HFE	Gelston, David, 12/23/1807, age 32.	V
266 HFE	Howell, Sylvanus, 2/16/1814, age 40.	V
267 HFE	Howell, Benjamin M., son of Silvanus & Mary, 12/12/1802, age 1.	V
268 HFE	Howell, James Boyles, son of Silvanus & Mary, 4/12/1807, age 2.	V
269 H	Fordham, Charles, 12/24/1843, age 39.	V
270 HF	Woodward, Caleb, 10/4/1804, age 46.	V
271 HF	Woodward, Mary, dau of Caleb & Chloe 3/20/1802, age 1.	V
272 HF	L'Hommedieu _____, son son of Charles & Sally, 4/25/1801, infant.	V
273 HFE	Stuart, Roxana, wife of Nathan 7/10/1804, age 18.	V
274 HFE	Fordham, Jane, wife of Capt. John N and infant, 4/6/1799, age 40.	V

275　F　　　footstone　　　unknown
276　F　　　footstone　　　"H.F"
277　HE　　Cooper, Henry, son of Thomas & Harriot
　　　　　　3/4/1803, infant.　　　　　　　　　　　UN

Grid # 9

278　HE　　Jones, Mary C., dau of Capt. William
　　　　　　& Charity, 9/5/1830, age 1.　　　　　　V
279*　HFE　Fordham, John N., 3/1/1808, age 53.　　V
280　HE　　Fordham, Julia Ann, dau of John N.
　　　　　　& Jane, 12/2/1821, age 26.　　　　　　V
281　HFE　Norton, Sophia, wife of Capt. Thomas
　　　　　　7/12/1824, age 49.　　　　　　　　　V
282　HFE　Norton, Capt. Thomas, 3/24/1822, age 58.　V
283　H　　 Havens, Henry Tho., son of Henry B.
　　　　　　& Hannah S., 1/4/1815, age 1.　　　　 V
284　H　　 Havens, Silas Sayre, son of Henry B. &
　　　　　　Hannah S., 5/1/1815, age 1.　　　　　 V
285　H　　 Havens, Elizabeth Wickham, dau of Henry B.
　　　　　　& Hannah S., 6/7/1827, age 2.　　　　 V
286　HFE　Perkins, Mary Gates, dau of Erastus &
　　　　　　Mary, 12/11/1828, age 1.　　　　　　 T
287　HF　 Wade, Jared, 5/6/1849, age 71.　　　　 V
288　HF　 Wade, Catharine, widow of Jared
　　　　　　6/19/1868, age 82.　　　　　　　　　V
289　H　　 Wade, Charles G., son of Jared &
　　　　　　Catharine, 12/11/1847, age 24.　　　　V
290　HE　　Wade, Lucetta Augusta, dau of Jared &
　　　　　　Catharine, 10/21/1837, age 4.　　　　 V
291　H　　 base for Wade, Charles R., son of Jared
　　　　　　& Catharine, 8/13/1822, age 6.　　　　V
292　H　　 Wade, unnamed son of Jared & Catharine
　　　　　　10/8/1807, infant.　　　　　　　　　V
293　HFE　Partridge, Charles Henry, son of Asa &
　　　　　　Betsey, 3/2/1827, age 29.　　　　　　V
294　HE　　Partridge, Betsey Conklin, wife of Asa

		10/25/1851, age 76.	V
295	HFE	**Partridge, Asa**, 12/10/1854, age 92.	V
296	H	**Smith, Benjamin**, 12/22/1836, age 66.	V
297	HF	**Smith, Desire** , wife of Benjamin	
		6/20/1817, age 42.	V
298	HE	**Sheffield, Betsey Maria**, dau of Isaac	
		& Betsey, 9/18/1803, age 2.	V
299	HFE	**Parker, Mary Abigail**, wife of Capt.	
		William, 7/11/1807, age 26.	V
300	HF	**Parker**, un-named dau of William &	
		Mary, 3/5/1807, infant.	V
301	F	footstone "NP", possibly for **Nancy Parker**	
302	HE	**Parker, Nancy**, wife of Abraham	
		1/8/1813, age 26.	V

Grid # 10

303	HE	**Lesliuce, John Sherman**, son of David &	
		Esther, 11/5/1832, age 1.	V
		(Leisheur and Leishure in the Church Records)	
304	HF	**Bridges, Geo. Washington**, son of William	
		& Phillis, 7/1/1829, age 23.	V
305	HFE	**Sayre, Margaret**, 12/21/1832, age 86.	V
306	F	footstone with no initials	
307	HE	**Raynor, Nancy Sayre**, wife of George	
		3/26/1817.	UN
308	H	**Raynor**, unnamed, 3/12/1817, infant.	UN
309	HFE	**Collins, Rebecca**, wife of Samuel	
		10/5/1820, age 26.	V
310	HE	**Collins, Luther Halsey**, son of Samuel	
		& Eliza, 7/12/1833, age 3.	V
311	H	**Pierson, Bathsheba**, widow of Job	
		11/25/1843, age 73.	V
312	H	**Collins, Elizabeth**, wife of Samuel	
		4/12/1850, age 49.	V
313	H	**Collins, Samuel**, 11/1/1868, age 73.	V

314	HFE	Franklin, Frederick, 11/15/1828, age 62.	V
315	HFE	Rogers, James H., son of Mary, 5/30/1829	
		infant.	UN
316	HFE	Kendrick, Mary, wife of Thomas	
		5/21/1833, age 66.	UN
317	H	Edwards, Albert, son of Elihu &	
		Elizabeth, 9/3/1807, infant.	V
318	HFE	Edwards, Elihu, 3/2/1820, age 46.	V
319	HFE	Edwards, Elizabeth, widow of Elihu	
		1/6/1850, age 71.	V
320	HFE	Edwards, Saumel, 10/27/1832, age 49.	V
321	HE	Corey, Abraham, 2/3/1845, age 82.	V
322	HF	Corey, Abraham Jr., 3/29/1845, age 43.	V
324	H	Mitchell, Virginia, dau of Nathan &	
		Mary Ann, 5/12/1829, age 2.	V
325	H	support stone which braced a former headstone	
325	H	Mitchell, John Carrol, son of Nathan &	
		Mary Ann, 3/17/1832, age 2.	V
326	H	Rogers, Enoch, son of Harvey & Phebe	
		10/23/1812, age 1.	V
327	HE	Halsey, Sarah, wife of Eliphalet	
		11/1/1818, age 24.	V
328	HFE	Halsey, Sarah, dau of Eliphalet & Sarah	
		9/24/1834, age 19.	V
		(stone signed J. Hiller, N.C. Ct)	
329	HE	Roberts, Roberts, 4/8/1846, age 42.	V
330	HF	Roberts, Esther, widow of Robert	
		1/30/1857, age 71.	V
331	HFE	Havens, Robert. son of Samuel & Esther	
		3/2/1827, age 16.	V
332	HFE	Hasbrook, Mary, wife of Alfred	
		10/9/1836, age 28.	V
333	H	Davis, Sylvester, 9/10/1843, age 21.	V

(Stone # 334 Nathaniel Mott can be found in grid #4)

BURIALS REMOVED TO OAKLAND CEMETERY
(From the Madison Street side of the OBG)

Babcock, Benjamin Sr., died July 2, 1839, age 66.

Baker, Nathan J., son of Captain John & Hannah Baker. Killed by a fall from the yard arm of the schooner, *Herald,* in Charleston, Massachusetts on June 7, 1839, age 20 years, 11 months, 24 days.

Beebe, Frances, wife of Lester Beebe, Jr., and daughter of Peleg Latham. Died March 12, 1829, age 29.

Beers, Alfred W., drowned near Greenport, Long Island, October 26, 1833, age 20 years, 6 months, 12 days.

Beers, Edward W., died August 2, 1822, age 6 years, 3 months.

Benjamin, James, died February 9, 1833, age 36.

Benjamin, Nancy L., relict of James Benjamin, died August 9, 1840, age 46.

Biglow, Anna Maria, wife of Horatio Biglow and daughter of Thomas P. & Mary Ripley, died June 1, 1816, age 23.

Byram, Betsey, daughter of Eliab & Cynthia Byram, died October 7, 1800, age 1 year, 3 months.

Byram, Charles C., son of Eliab & Cynthia Byram, died November 6, 1801, age 1 year, 8 months.

Budd, Joshua, died at Port au Prince, S.D., March 13, 1820, age 53.

Budd, Betsey Ann, daughter of Captain Joshua & Phebe Budd, died September 12 1833, age 38.

Cook, Nathan, consort of Mary Cook and son of T. & P. Cook, died November 7, 1811, age 22.

Cooper, Abigail, wife of Caleb, died May 13, 1840, age 89.

Cooper, Caleb, died April 16, 1834, age 89.

Corey, son and daughter of Phenehas & Nancy Corey, born and died April 17, 1800, along with two other children.

Corey, William H., son of Phenehas & Nancy Corey, died February 23, 1800, age 2.

Crowell, Sarah, daughter of Samuel & Sarah L'Hommedieu Crowell, died June 15, 1830, age 41.

Edwards, Russell, died April 7, 1836, age 58.

Eldredge, Deacon Abner, died January 14, 1840, age 73.

Eldredge, Mary, wife of James Eldredge, died July 6, 1809, age 26.

Eldredge, William F., son of J. & E. Eldredge, age 19. Died while fighting the memorable fire of August 11, 1838 in Sag Harbor.

Fordham, Daniel B., son of Captain Peletiah & Maria Fordham, died April 19, 1833, age 21, along with two other children.

Fordham, Frances, daughter of William B. & Mary Fordham, died December 29, 1809, age 7 months.

Fordham, Harriet Havens, died September 9, 1825.

Fordham, Harriet Lucretia, died January 7, 1832.

Fordham, James H., died October 9, 1828.

Fordham, Jarus, died July 24, 1831, age 64.

Fordham, Mary, widow of Jarus Fordham, died November 3, 1852, age 80.

Fordham, Mary, wife of William B. Fordham, died December 5, 1809, age 27.

Fordham, Mary, wife of Captain Nathan Fordham, died November 2, 1818, age 57, along with seven children.

Fordham, Mary E., died November 9, 1839.

Fordham, Captain Nathan, died July 7, 1838, age 80.

Fordham, Robert, died February 27, 1834, age 43.

Fordham, Sarah L., died November 9, 1840.

Fordham, William B., died June 14, 1866, age 86.

Fosdick, Sylvester, consort of Harriet R. and a son of Richard & Phebe Fosdick, died 1826 or 1833.

Fosdick, Harriet R., daughter of Silas & Mary Raymond, died January 30, 1844, age 48.

Fosdick, Thomas Richard, son of Richard & Phebe Fosdick of Cincinnati. Born June 22, 1797 at New London and died at Sag Harbor, August 1, 1829.

Fowler, Desire L., wife of Captain Oliver Fowler, died December 16, 1828, age 53.

Fowler, Oliver, son of Samuel & Nancy Nickels Fowler, died March 12, 1820, age 4 months, 13 days.

Gardiner, Frances M., wife of Rev. John D. Gardiner, died March 23, 1814, age 33.

Gardiner, James Madison, born at Chester, New Jersey and died at Sag Harbor April 3, 1836, age 26 years, 1 month, 17 days.

Glover, Captain Alfred, master of the ship, *Acasta,* of Sag Harbor, who was killed by the blow of a whale in the South Atlantic Ocean, January 14, 1835, age 29 years, 6 months.

Glover, Mary, daughter of Benjamin & Mary Glover, died April 14, 1815, age 16 years, 3 months.

Green, Captain Henry & Roxanna's "Two children of my

daughter's, died 1833 and 1839.

Hallock, Fanny Maria, wife of Charles Hallock, died December 14, 1827, age 21 years, 8 months.

Hand, Charlotte, wife of David Hand, died March 20, 1800, age 30.

Halsey, Sylvanus, died July 5, 1833, age 47.

Hand, Captain David, Died February 29, 1840, age 84.

Hand, Hannah, wife of David Hand, died October 18, 1798, age 30.

Hand, Hannah, wife of David Hand, died April 1, 1835, age 60.

Hand, Hannah Jane, daughter of Captain David & Julia Ann Hand, died August 22, 1834, age 1 year, 5 months, 29 days.

Hand, Julia Abigail, daughter of Captain David & Julia Ann Hand, died September 1, 1838, age 1 year, 6 months.

Hand, Mary, wife of David Hand, died July 12, 1794, age 32.

Hand, Sarah L., wife of Timothy P. Hand, died April 7, 1831, age 27.

Hand, Susannah, wife of David Hand, died October 10, 1791, age 27.

Havens, Abigail Tiley, widow of Dr. Jonathan Havens, died September 5, 1820, age 85.

Havens, Bethiah, wife of Captain William Havens, died December 14, 1830, age 75.

Havens, Cynthia Stanton, widow, died June 6, 1851, age 73.

Havens, Gabriel, son of Dr. Jonathan & Abigail, died April 7, 1839, age 72.

Havens, Dr. Jonathan, son of Constant & Abigail Havens, died April 26, 1801, age 64.

Havens, Nathaniel T., died March 24, 1829, age 57 years, 7 months.

Havens, Ptolmey, son of Dr. Jonathan & Abigail Havens, died November 3, 1798, age 19.

Hedges, three children of Job & Mary B. Hedges, 1819-1827.

Hedges, Jesse, died May 28, 1826, age 55.

Hedges, Naomi & George B., wife and son of Jesse Hedges who were drowned in the packet of Captain N.F. Sayre which sunk in a gale of wind on the night of October 7, 1826, on a passage from Sag Harbor to New York. She was 57, her son, 15. Also other children.

Hill, Isabel, wife of Ithuel Hill, died October 29,1839, age 71, also children.

Howell, James, born in Southampton October 15, 1731. One of the earliest settlers at Sag Harbor. He kept a house that stood on the present site of the American Hotel as a tavern, and there the officers commanding the British garrison had headquarters during the Revolutionary War. He died December 12, 1808.

Howell, Lucretia, consort of James Howell, died November 14, 1791, age 51, and 5 children who died 1767, 1775, 1791, 1800.

Howell, Matthew, died April 13, 1825, age 61 years, 2 months, 21 days.

Jarvis, David S., drowned near Greenport, October 26, 1833, age 27 years, 20 days.

Latham, Eleazer, son of Captain Peleg & Matsey Latham, died August 28, 1793, age 2 years, 28 days.

Latham, Matsey, wife of Captain Peleg Latham, died March 22, 1825, age 57. Also a son who died August 13, 1798.

Latham, Captain Peleg, died June 25, 1833.

Lawton, Frances Mary, wife of Dr. Elijah L. Lawton, and only daughter of of E.& R. Sage, buried in Mobile, Alabama with her husband. Stone to their memory erected in Oakland Cemetery. She died September 25, 1819, age 27. He died ten days later.

L'Hommedieu, Charity, daughter of Samuel & Sarah L'Hommedieu, died October 25, 1788, age 8.

L'Hommedieu, Elizabeth, of Southold, died November 6, 1798, age 95.

L'Hommedieu, Samuel, born in Southold, died at Sag Harbor, March 7, 1834, age 91.

L'Hommedieu, Sarah, wife of Samuel L'Hommedieu, died November 18, 1822, age 70.

Loper, two children of Silas and Sarah Loper, died in 1839.

Lowen, Nancy, widow, died April 1, 1889. age 99.

Lowen, William, died September 1, 1828, age 38.

Mitchell, Betsey, relict of Captain John Mitchell, died September 23, 1833, age 44.

Mitchell, Captain Jno., died October 25, 1826, age 58.

Munsell, Reverend Jabez, died at Norfolk, Virginia, August 1, 1832, age 60.

Pierson, James, died September 20, 1838, age 56.

Prentice, Dr. Amos, died May 9, 1827, age 57.

Prentice, Lucinda, his widow, died May 17, 1849, age 73.

Price, Abigail, widow of John Price, died March 19, 1860, age 84.

Price, James H., son of James H. and Deborah K. Price, died

September 16, 1839, age 2 years, 4 months, 22 days.

Price, Captain John Price, died August 14, 1809, age 40.

Raymond, George R., son of Silas and Mary Raymond, died December 19, 1832.

Raymond, Mary, widow, died April 29, 1844, age 72.

Raymond, Silas, died May 19, 1835, age 69.

Raymond, William, died July 23, 1827, age 66.

Ripley, John C., son of John C. and Mary Ripley, died March 27, 1814, age 18.

Ripley, Maria, consort of Mr. Thomas P. Ripley, died July 14, 1800, age 29.

Rose, Frances and Rose, Henry M., daughter and son of Christopher and Morgiana Rose, died 1835 and 1837.

Russell, Sarah, wife of David Russell, died June 22, 1816, age 68.

Sage, Dr. Ebenezer, born at Chatham, Connecticut, died Sag Harbor, January 20, 1834, age 79.

Sage, Ruth, wife of Dr. Sage, died May 9, 1831, near the end of her 67th year.

Sayre, Hannah, wife of Captain Jeremiah Sayre and daughter of Captain David Hand, died November 18, 1834, age 25.

Schellinger, Daniel, died February 1, 1835, age 50.

Slate, Rachel, wife of Oliver Slate, died December 29, 1806, age 25.

Slate, Rachel, daughter of Oliver & Rachel Slate, died February 21, 1823, age 6 years, 3 months.

Sleight, Deacon Augustus, died June 28, 1830, age 46.

Sleight, Mehetable, wife of Deacon Augustus Sleight, died at Sandy Hill, New York, December 3, 1824, age 40.

Street, Nancy M., relict of Henry Street, died September 23, 1828, age 31.

Tabor, Nancy, wife of Pardon Tabor, died November 15, 1815, age 35, also two children.

Terry, David P., son of Joshua & Clarissa Terry. Officer on the ship, *Sabrina,* who was struck by a whale off the Crosettes, December 25, 1841, and who died December 27, 1841, age 24.

Wade, Bathsheba M., wife of Jared Wade Jr. who died March 19, 1843, age 25. "She died while her husband was at sea."

Wentworth, Frances, wife of Josiah Wentworth, died June 22, 1835, age 74.

Westfall, Newton E., a native of Virginia, died May 27, 1833, age 47.

Wolf, Mary F.D., died December 22, 1843, age 20.

EPITAPHS

The following epitaphs are inscribed on stones in the Old Burying Ground. The grid and stone numbers are given to help locate them.

Grid # 1

#2 **William and John Hatfield**, sons of Smith and Catherine Hatfield (who drowned in Gardiner's Bay, off the Fire Place Point by the swamping of a sail boat, September 12, 1843. Ten days afterwards their bodies were found and brought to Sag Harbor for burial).
"Put thy trust in no man in the hour of danger, for when these boys were drowned man fled from the rescue."

#3 **Sally Crowell**, wife of Asa
"From cares and fears & piercing pain
She's fled to joys above.
Nor do we wish her to return
Nor may we court her love.
But while we view this lonely place
And read thy virtues o'er,
We ne'er shall see thee more."

#5 **Mary Hedges**, wife of Jeremiah
"In the various relations of life
she discharged her duties with
fidelity to herself, her family,
her neighbors, and her God.
She died in peace with the
firm hope of everlasting glory
beyond the grave."

#13 **Benjamin Price**
"Blessed are the dead which
die in the Lord."

#18   Emeline Ives, wife of E.R. Ives
"Here enthroned in the cold embrace of earth
sleeps the Loved Emeline, wife of E.R. Ives."
"She sleeps, but the clods of earth
press on her lov'd bosom but light."

#19   Sally Roberts, age 10
"This stone is inscribed in memory of Sally Roberts
as a testimony of her promising usefulness
to them she serv'd."
"Death is at best a vain precarious thing,
and fair faced youth is ever on the wing."

#21   Ephraim Niles, son of Peleg and Phebe
"Behold and see as you pass by
As you are now so once was I
As I am now so you must be
Prepare for death and follow me."

#22   George Niles
"Tho Boreas wind and Neptune's wave
Hath tossed me to and fro,
By God's decree you plainly see
I'm harbored here below."

#25   Timothy Corniell, son of Stephen and Prigtel
"Can this tender prince be
passing by
Children like buds before
They bloom, may die."

#28   Egbert Smith, son of Stephen and Catherine
"This lovely boy (illegible)
call'd early by (illegible) doom
Just came to show
how sweet a flower
In Paradise could bloom."

#29 **Susannah Welden**, dau. of Jonathan and Mehitabel
"Happy the babe
who privileged by fate
to shorter labours & a
lighter weight
Receiv'd but yesterday
the gift of breath."

#30 **Abigail Jagger**, relict of Captain William
"With love her soul was fir'd
Triumphant she expired,
To meet her God above
In realms of peace and love."

#32 **Benjamin Jagger**, son of William and Abigail
"No age nor sex can death defy
Think mortal what it is to die."

Grid # 2

#34 **Mary Ann Godbee**, dau. of John and Lydia
"Hark, hear the sweet refrain
From the heart
Prepare my friends to meet
Your hastening doom.
When death arrives you must
Obey its call
Father, Mother, Brothers,
Sisters, Lovers, all."

#36 Broken half of stone, Person unknown.
"Tho so early in this lonely spot
Thy wasted form was doom'd to lie,
Its mouldering dust won't be forgot
when Jesus comes from yonder sky
This body then his call shall hear
and rise from its imprisoned clay
to soar above this changing sphere
and live in one eternal day."

#41   **Mary Youngs**, dau. of David and Mary
(illegible)

#45   **Mehitable L'Hommedieu**, wife of Capt. Ephraim
"Stop reader shed a mournful tear
Upon the dust which slumbers here
And while you read the fate of me
Think on the glass that runs for thee."

#47   **John Peirson & Nathaniel Baker**
"This stone erected by their fellow citizens
is a tribute of respect to the memory of
Nath'l Baker & John Peirson who were
unfortunately killed in this place Feb. 23, 1815,
by the accidental discharge of a cannon
while celebrating the return of peace between
the U. States & G. Britain. Their ages 22 years."

#51   **David Bates**, son of Capt. Isachar and Hannah
"My Saviour now
Enthroned on high
Rose from the grave
And so shall I
For where he is
There I must be."

#53   **Jemima Brown**, wife of Capt. David
"An infant of Capt. David and Jemima Brown
ae 1, lies buried by her side."

#54   **Captain David Brown**
"As he lived revered and respected
he died lamented by all equally."

#55   **Phebe K. Edwards**, wife of Silas W.
"So fair, so young, so gentle, so sincere,
so lovely, so early lost, may claim a tear.
We mourn not, if the life resumed by Heaven
was to every end for which 'twas given."

#56   **Mary Latham**, wife of Daniel
"In youthful bloom I was cut off
My frame of mortal clay
May rest awhile until I come
To everlasting day."

#57   **Emmeline Latham**, dau. of Daniel and Mary
"The unrelenting hand of death
Has closed her eyes, has stopt her breath.
Nor youth nor tender love could save
The darling from the op'ning grave."

#58   **Alden Spooner**, son of Alden and Rebecca
"A son more pleasant to a parents eye
Sure ne'er to mortals fondest hope was given,
Awhile his Maker lent the lovely boy,
But called him early to his native Heaven."

#64   **Rebecca Clark**, wife of Captain Moses
"Husband and children all farewell
I sleep above and with you dwell
Jesus calls and I must go
From this world of sin and woe."

#65   **William Mulford Leek**, son of Jacob and Harriet
"Sick of a life precluding
so much pain,
He chose to give it back
to God again."

Grid # 3

#69   **Lester Beebe**, son of Captain Thomas and Nancy
"God of eternity from thee
Did infant time his being draw
Moments and days and months and years
Revolve by thy unvaried law.
Silent and slow they glide away
Stately and strong the current flows

Lost in eternity's wide sea
The boundless gulf from which it rose."

#70   **Captain Thomas Beebe**
        (illegible)

#71   **Nancy Beebe**, wife of Capt. Thomas
"Happy soul thy days are ended
All thy mourning days below
God by angels guards attended
To the sight of Jesus go.
Waiting to receive thy spirit
Lo the Savior shouts above
Show the glory of his merit
Reaches out the crown of love.
For the joy he sets before thee
Bear a momentary pain
Dies to live the life of glory
Suffer with thy hand to reign."

#72   **Alletta Beebe**, wife of Jason
"The once loved form now cold & dead
Each mournful thought imploys
And nature weeps her comfort fled
And shattered all her joys.
Cease then fond nature cease thy tears
The Savior dwells on high
There unrelenting spring appears
There joys shall never die."

#73   **Jason Beebe**, son of Capt. Lester and Bethiah
"Till the last hour of life thy loss we'll mourn
and show thy grace with tears of sorrow shed,
O may we then on angels wings be bourne
to see him live, who now alas is dead.
We mourn thy sudden swift remorse
from each and all enjoyments here.
When Christ commands we must obey
without a murmur or a tear."

#74   **Edgar Fowler Fordham,** son of Frederick and
Samantha
"For of such is the kingdom of heaven."

#75   **George Frederick Fordham**, son of Frederick and
Samantha
"Suffer little children to come unto me."

#77   **Mary Ann Coles**, dau. of Phebe and Thaddeus
"Sleep on sweet babe and find thy rest,
God call'd thee home, He thought it best."

#80   **Hugh G. Fordham**
"It is but a just tribute of respect to
his memory to say that in all the relations
of life which he sustained, he was truly an
amiable and excellent man.
He lived respected by all men
And universally honored."

#81   **Latham Fordham**
"The eye of him that hath seen me
Shall see me no more.
Thine eyes are upon me and
I am not."
          Job: Chapter 7 Verse 8

#82   **Sarah Eldredge**
          (illegible)

#85   **Sally Eldredge**, wife of Stillman
"Readers
Nothing is worth & thought beneath
But how you may escape the death
That never dies.
How make your own election sure."

Grid # 4

#89   **Charles Matthews**, son of Nathan and Betsey
"Sleep on sweet child and
take thy rest.
God call'd thee home, he
thought it best."

#90   **Betsey Matthews**, wife of Nathaniel (Nathan)
"This lonely place is dear to me
Tho over it no willows weep
For underneath its bowery sad
A companion's mould'ring ashes sleep."

#98   **Capt. Elkanah Smith**
        (illegible)

#99   **Elkanah Smith**
"Drowned on his passage rom New York
to Georgetown, South Carolina."
"In the midst of life and youthful bloom
He sunk to rest in ocean's deep
and there he found a watery tomb
and left his friends to weep."

#100   **Lucy Eldredge**, wife of William
"Her happy soul is free
Releas'd from mortal chains,
Has launched on that unbounded sea
Where Christ forever reigns."

#106   **Ruth B. Smith**, wife of Capt. Charles, Jr.
(8 lines, last 4 below are partially legible)
"shall this (illegible) would ring (illegible)
and mingle with the dust.
Till Jesus calls us to the sky
to shine among the just."

#107   **Theodore Bertrand Fordham**, son of George
        and Frances

"Drowned in Gardiner's Bay off the Fire Place Point
by the swamping of a sailboat, September 12, 1843."

#108   **Charles Dering Fordham**, son of George and Frances
(illegible)

Grid # 5

#111   **Priscilla Wood,** wife of Stephen D.
"There is a glorious rest
For weeping mortals given,
And when they sink on
Earth's cold breast
They find that rest in Heaven."

#116   **Brewster Miller**
"The noblest work of God
An honest man."

#117   **Tamos Tucker**
"Teach me the measure
of my days
thou author of my frame,
I would survey life's
innermost space
and learn how frail I am."

#118   **Abigail Smith**, dau. of Elias and Charlotte
"Ere sin could blight or sorrow fade
Death came with friendly care,
The opening bud to Heaven conveyed
And bade it blossom there."

#119   **Cynthia B. Lugar**, wife of George C.
"Thou art gone to thy final rest
Then why should my sould be so sad,
I know thou hast gone where the weary are blest
And the mourner looks up and is glad."

#122 **Caroline Prince**, wife of Simeon
"There is a glorious rest
For weeping mortals given,
And when they sink on
Earth's cold breast
They find that rest in Heaven."

#123 **Juan Antonio Dalosta** (Portuguese Sailor)
"Erected by his fellow countrymen."

#126 **Francisco Joze Goncalues Labanja**
        (Portuguese Sailor)
"Erected by his fellow countrymen."

#127 **Joachim Joze Panna** (Portuguese Sailor)
"Erected by his fellow countrymen."

#128 **Francisco Lucianni** (Portuguese Sailor)
"Erected by his fellow countrymen."

#129 **Manuel Francisco** (Portuguese Sailor)
"Fell from the mast on Ship Hannibal
July 24, 1833."
"Erected by his fellow countrymen."

#130 **Charles Snook**
"A kind husband, father and
friend. Our loss is deeply felt."

#133 **Samuel Oakley**
"Honored by all who knew him
Here sleeps the man in midst of life
Cut down in blooming youth
Who left to weep a mourning wife
and parents bath'd in tears,
from brothers, sisters purest love
from friendship's tenderest ties
God took his spirit far above
Earth's ever-changing skies."

#136   **Mehetabel Solomon**, wife of Samuel
"Draw near to hem and
Wipe off all your tears
I shall lie here till Christ appears,
And when he comes I hope to strive
Unto a life that never dies."

#140   **Lynus Russell**, son of John and Sarah
"The lovely son was called home
to dwell with spirits unknown."

#141   **Percey Scovill**
"Blessed are the dead
which die in the Lord."

#143   **Mariah Halsey**, dau. of Henry
"Suffer little children to come unto me,
for of such is the Kingdom of Heaven."

#144   **Phebe Ann Smith**, dau. of David and Phebe
"By this you see
no age is free
from sickness, pain and death."

#145   **Capt. Richard P. Beckwith**
       (illegible)

#146   **Mical C. Wiggins**
"Reader prepare, remember death is near
My time is past, eternity is here.
This speaking marble loud doth warn you all,
Youth, manhood, aged, to each a peaceful call."

#147   **James Wiggins**
"Ye sons of men will satisfaction know
God's own right hand dispenses all below.
No good nor evil does by chance befall
He reigns supreme and he directs us all."

#148   **Capt. Lewis Smith**
"Ah, but a just tribute to his memory,
to say that as a husband, a neighbor, and
citizen, he possessed all those qualities
of which rendered him esteemed and
respected by his friends and acquaintances."

#149   **Lettis Smith**, wife of Captain Lewis
"Life and the grave two different lessons give
Life teaches how to die, death how to live."

#150   **Obid Smith**
"In the various relations of life
he discharged his duties with fidelity
to himself, his family, his neighbors
and his God."

#151   **Mercey Smith**, wife of Obid
        (illegible)

#152   **Elizabeth D. Sherman**, widow of Baldwin
"I go to a new house where
there is no more trouble."

Grid # 6

#154   **John Nicoll Havens**, son of Silas and Proculah
"Behold, inscrib'd upon this stone
A pleasant babe an only son,
A father's grones and Mother's cries
Could not avail, so here he lies."
(note spelling of groans)

#155   **Cordela Havens**, dau. of Silas and Proculah
"No tender love nor innocence
Could save the little darling from
an untimely grave."

#156   **Proculah Havens**, dau. of Silas and Proculah
"Scarce liv'd the babe
The dawning day espied,
Before it droop'd as little
beads and died."

#157   **Hannah Gardiner**, wife of Jeremiah
(first four lines illegible)
"where in this land of rife (illegible)
thou had fought the fight (illegible)
or (illegible) up the prize
to triumph in yonder sky
in heaven thy happy home."

#158   **Henry L. Smith**
"This is the resting place
of one cut down in the midst of youth,
enterprise and hope. Affectionately
loved him to the last, with
her adornments and her tears.
She could do no more, and he fell
asleep in the hope of that religion
which had been his guide
in life, and his comfort
in sickness."   JAC (stonecutter's initials)

#159   **Elizabeth Smith**, wife of Joseph
(illegible)

#161   **Captain Joseph Smith**
"The winter of troubles is past
The storms of affliction are o'er
His struggle is ended at last
And sorrow and death are no more."

#162   **Hannah Foster**, wife of Peter
(illegible)

#163   **Capt. William Parker**
(illegible)

#164 Nancy Maria Parker, dau. of William and Phebe
"When those we love are from us torn
Tis meet that kindred hearts shall mourn.
Nor we fail the tear to shed
Ov'r her who slumbers with the dead.
Our daughter, sister, sleeps beneath
For her we wear the cypress wreath
While her bright spirit mounts the sky
To mingle with the blest on high."

#165 Capt. Henry Parker
(first 8 line illegible)
"Farewell dear friend. We leave thee
with thy Savior and thy God."

#167 Capt. Silas Sayre and Esther Sayre
"In life he was respected,
In death lamented.
Erected by an affectionate son and
brother of Charles D. Sayre."

#168 Wickham Sayre
"Tis thine O Death the sender we to read
of son, of brother and endearing friend.
Her Wickham (illegible) with (illegible)
He ne'er had met (illegible) grave
cease then to grieve (illegible) goodness thence,
He took but what he had reclaim'd his own."

#169 Jeremiah Sayre and David Sayre, Jr.
"Should this marble, reader, catch thine eye
Don't pass the solitary mansion bye;
There sleeps one brother whom his friends deplore
The other died on Georgia's distant shore,
Cut off in bloom they left the world behind
A friend and parent in their God to find."

#174 Nathan Sayre
"Who was drwoned on a passage

from this Port to New York
on the night of October 7, 1826, aged 52 years."

#177a **Andrew Satterly**, son of Capt. Stephen and Margaret
last line reads
"return to death."

#178   **Margaret Satterly**, relict of Capt. Stephen
"Farewell bright soul, a short farewell,
Till we shall meet again above
In the sweet groves where pleasures dwell
And trees of life bear fruits of love."

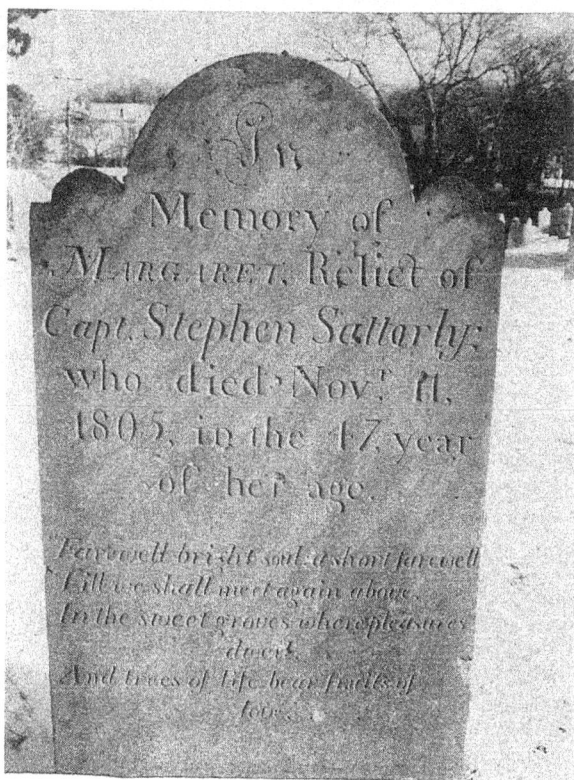

Margaret Satterly, stone # 178

#179 Thomas L. Harris and Henry D. Harris
"Who drowned in Gardiner's Bay, November 27, 1823,
ae 25 years. Remains were found on the beach near
3 Mile Harbor where they were interred July 17, 1824."

#180 Amma Harris, wife of Thomas Harris
(on children's stones mother's name is inscribed "Amy")
"This no more than paying a
just tribute to the memory of
this excellent woman. To say
that she was possessed of an eminent
degree of the virtue of a
Christian and devoted wife,
a kind neighbor to the extent of her
ability in time of sickness and plenty.
We said of her that as she lived, beloved in (illegible)
she died without an enemy and universally regretted."

#181 Lucretia S. Havens, dau. of Thomas and Amy
"Smile on the blooming bud
Death snatched her life away.
A soul returned to God
Her body to its native clay."

#182 Sarah Scott Harris, dau. of Thomas and Amy
"May this instruct my friends
No age from death is free."

#183 Katurah Harris, dau. of Thomas and Amy
"My friend has gone
and (part of stone missing) above."

#185 Josiah Hand
"Oh we have watched his parting breath
and close his weary eyes,
and sighed to see how sadly death
can sever human ties."

#188   **Charity Corey**, dau. of John and Phebe
"An evening bud
A morning flower
Cut down & withered
in an hour."

#190   **Austin Stuart**
(illegible)

#191   **Lucretia Pierson**, wife of Hervey
"Heaven gives us friends to
bless the present scene,
Resumes them to prepare
us for the new."

#192   **Abigail Stuart**, wife of Silas
"In the various relations of life
which she sustained, she adorned
the doctrines of the gospel.
She was an affectionate wife, a
tender mother, a faithful friend,
a pious and humble Christian."

#195   **Polly Stewart**, wife of Silas
(illegible)

#197   **John Chase**
"Stop traveller and know,
Death like a deluge sweeps
Us to the grave."

#201   **Samuel Fordham**
"Adieu my wife, sweet soother of my cares,
Adieu my babe, your loving father cries.
Beneath this stone my body sleeps in dust
My hopes in God I dwell among the skies."

Grid # 7

#205 **David Sherard**
"Stop readershed a mournful tear
Upon the dust which slumbers here
And while you read the fate of me
Think on the glass that runs for thee.
The eye of him that hath seen me
Shall see me no more, thine eyes are
Upon me and I am not."

#206 **John Goodwin, Jr.**
"Come all you friends as you pass by
Upon this vault you cast your eye,
Prepare for death for soon it will be,
Soon after this you follow me."

#207 **Nehemiah B. Cook**
"At his own request
Tho poor, he desired
to make many rich."

#208 **William Lester Hall**
"Died on a visit for benefit of his health
in Sag Harbor August 4, 1803 age 28.
He was a native of Great Britain, received
his education in the city of London, and
resided in the County of Effingham, in
the state of Georgia."

#210 **Nabby Hard** (or Hand), wife of Lemuel
          (Stonecutter may have mis-cut this stone)
"My dearest friends when
this my grave you see,
hear the cry, prepare
to follow me."

#216 **Sally Halsey**, wife of Job
"I bid adieu to all below
I go where Angels dwell.

Since tis God's will it shall be so,
I bid you all farewell."

#217   **Nancy Halsey**, wife of George
"Her piety was exceptional,
a testimonial consistent with
manifesting itself in all her
relations of life, leading her to rejoice
in adulation and to be patient in suffering in the end
and to meet the King of sorrow
with the smile of friendship
and hope of a blessed immortality."

#220   **Mehitabel Hildreth**, wife of Capt. Luther
"Farewell bright soul a short farewell
Till we shall meet again above
In the sweet groves where pleasures dwell
And trees of life bear fruits of Love."

#221   **Captain Luther Hildreth**
"To Heavens (illegible) will visions doth return
Be ere it noonday or in blooming morn,
But samll the difference when that summons given
Be prepared to tread the gates of Heaven."

#222   **Abigail Hildreth**, wife of Capt. Luther
"Till the last hour of general doom
May angels guard thy precious trust
To the cold chamber of her tomb
And keep secure her sleeping dust."

#223   **Hainulal Horton**, wife of Capt. J. Havens Horton
"No sighs nor tears nor weeping friends
could save,
The dear and lovely victim from
the grave.
Her patience and submission
surpast elucidation."

#224 **Henry Augustus Sleight,** son of Henry C. and
Cornelia
(illegible)

#225 **Luther Brown Hildreth,** son of Samuel and Phebe
(illegible)

#227 **Eliza Tully Whittlesey,** dau. of John and Sally
"Farewell my friends
Adieu to pain
My life was short
Death is gain."

#229 **Sarah Hobart,** wife of Benjamin
"Farewell dear partner, thou in earthly all,
Drest in dust and wait the trumpets call,
In this retreat wrapt in death's dismal gloom,
My sun rose fair but set ere it was noon,
Stop, stranger, stop and see how short my date
The silent tomb ere must be your fate."

#231 **Rebekah Foster,** dau. of Thomas and Rebekah
"My friends came see me as I lie
And know that you will surely die
Seek Heaven whilst you have your breath
And put not off the hour of Death."

#232 **Joseph W. Foster, Jr.**
"As for me, I will behold
thy face in righteousness.
I shall be satisfied when I awake
with thy likeness."
Psalms 17:15

#235 **Betsey Fordham,** wife of John
"Teach me to live that I may dread
the grave as little as my bed.
Teach me to die that so I may
Triumphing rise on the last day."

#237 **Charity Corey**, wife of Braddock
"I've found the pearl
of greater price
My Christ what shall I call
My Christ is first
My Christ is last
MyChrist is all in all."

#238 **Frances Boardman**, wife of Daniel
"Afflictions sore long time she bore
Physicians were in vain,
Till death gave ease and God did please
to free her from her pain."

#239 **Lydia Ripley**
"Glory be to God: his ways are just
And every (illegible) of life (or wife)
What (illegible) bodies sleep
(illegible) shall rife."
(parts of this stone have flaked off)

Grid # 8

#240 **Hettie Parker**
"Whosoever drinketh of the water that it shall fill him,
Shall never thirst."

#241 **Sally Hand**, wife of Isaac
(a sandstone gravestone paritally spalled. Last two lines read)
"Their spirit freed to world's unknown,
Reader prepare to follow on."

#243 **Abigail Fordham**, wife of Nathan (broken base)
(The epitaph was recorded by Louis Tooker Vail when he did
his inventory. The stone no longer exists).
"No more the thought which fills the mind with woe,
No more the tears of Keen sensation flow,
For while perhaps the hand of God we moan,
She swells the Anthem at her Father's throne."

#244   **Nathan and Sarah Fordham,** (broken stone and
base0 (illegible)

#248   **Hannah Parker,** wife of Capt. James H.
"And angels food were her repast
Devotion was her work
and thence she tried
delights which strangers never taste."

#249   **James Parker,** son of Capt. James H. and Hannah
"Even so them also which die
in Jesus will God bring with him."

#250   **Maria Sleight Higbie,** wife of Aaron H.
"Life's duty done, depart the day
and from its hand the spirit lay
While heaven & earth combine (illegible)
She lived the righteous (illegible)."

#256   **Henry Hildreth,** son of Capt. John and Christiana
(illegible)

#258   **Capt. John Hildreth**
"Milk and a swathe at first
our whole demand.
Our whole domain at last
A turf or stone."

#259   **Hugh Gelston**
"As a tribute of respect to the memory of Mr. Gelston,
justice to say that he was an affectionate husband,
a kind neighbor, a faithful friend, a Patriot, and
was all an honest men, the noblest work of God,
to such he was respected, beloved and
deplored to all who knew him."

#260   **Puah Gelston,** wife of Hugh
"Mrs. Gelston was for many years, a member
of the Presbyterian Church in this place, and

through her last protracted illness she enjoyed much of
the consolation of the Christian hope of Heaven,
hearing witness in the truths of the Gospel,
the doctrines of which she adorned
by an exemplary life and consolation."

#264 **Elizabeth Gelston**, wife of David
"For fifty years she tredded disconsolately in the path
of widowhood, nor seemed ever to forget him to whom
in early life she had wedded her earthly affections, but
who in a seemingly untimely hour had been suddenly
cut down a stroke of Providence that caused the throne
of reason to tremble to its very centre and despair and
sorrow to usurp the place of trust and repose even to
the end of her journey through life."

#265 **David Gelston**
"How lov'd, how chance avails the not
to whom related or by whom begot,
A heap of dust alone remains of thee
Tis all thou art and all the proud shall be."

#266 **Sylvanus Howell**
"Not all the tears of those I love
could keep my soul from Christ above,
from Jesus my best friend.
Hark, it's his Heavenly voice I hear
farewell my wife, my children dear,
my sorrows now shall end."

#267 **Benjamin M. Howell**, son of Silvanus and Mary
"Adieu my friends
Adieu to pain,
My life was short
But death is gain."

#268 **James Boyles Howell**, son of Silvanus and Mary
"Farewell sweet babe
go take thy rest.

Recline thy head
On Jesus breast."

#273 **Roxana Stuart**, wife of Nathan
"Arise dear soul
and take thy heavenly flight,
Thru the dark regions
of the gloomy night.
The start will all their light display
to guide thee onward
to eternal day."

#274 **Jane Fordham**, wife of Capt. John M.
"Calm and serene She yields her mortal breath
In hope of Bliss she triumphs over Death,
In vain the Billows of death Jordan roll
To crown and overwhelm her pious soul."

#277 **Henry Cooper**, son of Thomas and Harriot
"Happy the babe who privileged by fate
to shorter labours & a lighter weight.
Receiv'd but yesterday the gift of breath."

Grid # 9

#278 **Mary C. Jones**, dau. of Capt. William and Charity
"Suffer little children to
come unto me and forbid
them not, for of such is
the Kingdom of Heaven."

#279 **John N. Fordham**
(illegible)

#280 **Julia Ann Fordham**, dau. of John and Jane
"Youth stay thy glee, turn hence thine eye
Learn how to live, know you must die,
Age mark me well, how thin the thread
One moment and the grave's thy bed."

#281 **Sophia Norton**, wife of Capt. Thomas
"As far removed from life's
All suffering woes,
Beneath this block her moldering limbs repose.
Her troubles cease, the weary are at rest,
Our Jusus saved twas God Almighty blest."

#282 **Capt. Thomas Norton**
"Saved from care and pain
and all the ills and strife,
(illegible) kind (illegible) and
Joy of my life."
(rest of epitaph is illegible).

#286 **Mary Gates Perkins**, dau. of Erastus and Mary
"Dear lovely babe repose in peace,
Now all thy worldly sorrows cease
No more the rude convulsions make
Thy little frame shall no more shake."

#290 **Lucetta Augusta Wade**, dau. of Jared and
Catharine
"So fades the lovely blooming flower
Find smiling solace of an hour.
So soon our transient comforts fly
And pleasures only bloom to die."

#293 **Charles Henry Partridge**, son of Asa
"In Remembrance of Charles Henry Partridge, only
son of Asa Partridge, Esq. who died at San Jose in
the Republic of Costa-Rica formerly the Kingdom
of Central America."
"He died in a foreign land but he died
with resignation and with hope."

#294 **Betsey Conklin Partridge**, wife of Asa
"In memory of Betsey Partridge, wife of Asa
Partridge, born long a resident in this place and who
died in the city of New York."
"Blessed are the dead which die in the Lord."

Rev. XIV, 13

"And hast bourne and hast patience and for my name's sake
and hath laboured and has not fainted."

Rev. II, 3

#295 Asa Partridge
"Who was born in Preston, Conn. lived in Sag Harbor
nearly 70 years and died in the city of New York.
And when they came that were hired, about the
eleventh hour they received every man a penny."

Matthew XX, 10

#298 Betsey Maria Sheffield, dau. of Isaac and Betsey
"Ah why so short
The flow'r appears
Strays the brief blossom
from the veil of tears.
Death received the treasure
to the deserts given
Claimed the fair forever, and
planted in Heaven."

#299 Mary Abigail Parker, wife of Capt. William
"Saved from sin and pain and all the ills of life,
Here rests a tender mother & a virtuous wife.
Sleep on Angelic saint thy maker's will obey,
Then rise again unchanged and mount to endless day."

#302 Nancy Parker, wife of Abraham
"Affliction sore long time I bore,
Physicians were in vain,
Till death did ease and God did please
to free me from my pain."

#303 John Sherman Lesliuce, son of David and Esther
"Sleep on sweet babe and take your rest,
God call'd you home, he thought it best."

Grid # 10

#305   **Margaret Sayre**
(illegible)

#306   **William Sayre**
(illegible)

#307   **Nancy Sayre Raynor**
(illegible)

#309   **Rebecca Collins**, wife of Samuel
"Come thy best of (illegible)
over thy (illegible) of values
And mourns with all the
(illegible) that he called
The fate of her who lies beneath
How happy those who early died
And lie reposing by the side
While we our parent from us torn
Are left to weep, lament and mourn."

#310   **Luther Halsey Collins**, son of Samuel and Eliza
"See here what cruel
death hath done.
Here sleeps in death an
only son.
Parents bleeding hearts
now say
The Lord both gave and
took away."

#314   **Frederick Franklin**
"The wound that's made where
death the knot unties,
no one knows but those
who realize."

#315   **James H. Rogers**, son of Mary
"I take these little lambs said he

and lay them on my breast,
Protection they shall find in me,
In me be ever blest."

#316 **Mary Kendrick**, wife of Thomas
"I'm home dear children, dry up your tears,
I must lie here till Christ appears."

#319 **Elizabeth (Betsey) Edwards**, widow of Elihu
"His life was gentle and serene his mind,
His morals pure, in every action just,
A husband dear and as a parent, kind,
As such he lies lamented in the dust."

#320 **Samuel Edwards**
"Short was thy passing
through this world of woe
To the bright realms of bliss
to which the righteous go
But soon we hope to meet
when this short life is o'er
To the bright world above
where parting is no more."

#321 **Abraham Cory**
(illegible)

#327 **Sarah Halsey**, wife of Eliphalet
(illegible)

#328 **Sarah Halsey**, dau. of Eliphalet and Sarah
"As she lived beloved & spiritual, so she died
Imortaled by all who knew her
With the love of Christ in her heart,
the love of Heaven in her eye, she fell
silently asleep in death only to awake
to Immortality & life beyond the grave."
                              J. Ritter N.H. Ct.

#329   **Robert Roberts**
"Oh death how hidden was thy visit paid
Scarce had I warning of thy fatal blow
To pitying friends who view where I am laid
Under the earth with sympathetic love."

#330   **Esther Roberts,** widow of Robert
"Rest in Peace."

#331   **Robert E. Havens,** son of Samuel and Esther
"End your weeping, Oh dry those tears
I have pass'd the gulph of pain and tears."

#332   **Mary Hasbrook,** wife of Alfred
"The wound that's made where
death the knot unties,
no one knows but those
who realize."

HELPFUL HINTS
"Reading Inscriptions More Easily"

After the gravestone has been cleaned of all lichens and mold,
it may still be very difficult to read names, dates and epitaphs. To bring
out the inscriptions more clearly, apply a layer of mud to marble or
other light colored stones, then gently wipe off the excess with a wet
sponge leaving the mud in the grooves of the words. You'll be
surprised how much easier the words will be to read. This process will
not harm the stone, but remember to wash off all traces of the mud
when you are finished, and leave the stone in a clean condition.

Sally Halsey, stone # 216

THE REVOLUTIONARY WAR PATRIOTS

Sag Harbor's Revolutionary War Patriots emigrated to Connecticut after the Battle of Long Island, August 26, 1776 left them at the mercy of the enemy. They took their families and belongings and stayed for the entire seven years the British occupied Long Island. Some took their ships and outfitted them as "Privateers" to harass the British shipping. **Captain William Havens**, interred in the Old Burying Ground, entered the Privateer Service in June 1778 as commander of the sloop, *Beaver*, a vessel of twelve 3 pounders and wreaked havoc on the British. Others left to escape the consequences of signing the Articles of Association in 1775 which in essence stated that the salvation of the rights and liberties of America depended on the firm union of its inhabitants and vigorous prosecution of the measures necessary for its safety. The signers resolved never to become slaves and adopt whatever it would take to preserve the Constitution and oppose the arbitrary and oppressive acts of the British Parliament until a reconciliation between Great Britain and America could be obtained. It was dated May 1775, Southampton.

THE REVOLUTIONARY WAR "PRISON SHIPS"

Long Island: Our Story, claims that more Americans died on the prison ships during the Revolution than in battle, and their statistics are quite likely. Among the thousands who died on these ships were a handful of local men who spent time on the prison ships of Wallabout Bay, Brooklyn. It would be noteworthy enough to tell the forgotten story of Sag Harbor's, **Frederic Fordham,** the militia captain's teenage son whose stone refers to his stay on the Wallabout ships. But when the legendary **David Hand** is found to be among the other prisoners, the men who experienced the prison ships and are buried in Wallabout Bay must also be discussed.

There are few besides the British of the 18th century, with their tradition of overcrowded jails and corrupt office holders, that could develop something so heinous as a prison ship. In 1776 the British brought this earlier English tradition to New York. They were acquiring more American prisoners than they could possibly imagine what to do with, and took their rotting, slimy hulks of dilapidated ships and crowded thousands of prisoners onto them. On the *Jersey*, a former 64 gun ship and one of the worst, there were more than a thousand prisoners, and the death toll estimated by historians to be seven to eight thousand men and women.

When conditions on the ships are examined, the high death toll is easy to understand. The hulks were beached on the sands of Wallabout Bay and the odor so bad that nearby farmers left their farms to avoid the stench. But the smell was the least of the problems. They had no shelter from the elements, being that the windows were only covered with bars. Prisoners rarely had clothes and many were just as naked as their comrades in Valley Forge and Morristown. Food consisted mainly of a wormy biscuit a day and wormy meat every few days, and the small amount of water allotted to them was usually dirty.

The prison commandant, William Cunningham, was described as blood-thirsty and sadistic even by men like the vicious Colonel (Bloody-Ban) Tarleton. When one considers how these men were notorious for ordering their soldiers to bayonet surrendered men and corpses five times, it is hard to imagine how much more of a monster Cunningham must have been. He thought nothing of ordering savage beatings and would set the guards on prisoners who found any excuse to celebrate or cook their wormy meat over a fire. His men greeted their charges in the morning screaming, "Rebels, turn out your dead!" Prisoners were known to go insane and knew to listen for warnings like, "madman with a knife!" in the middle of the night.

On the prison ships where the average life span was about three months, it's miraculous how **Frederic Fordham**, only sixteen when he died in 1732, survived two years, and got one of the rare exchanges. Frederic was sick with a fever at the time of his exchange, but managed to make the long trek across war-torn Long Island to Sag Harbor. Two weeks after he arrived home he died from the sickness he acquired during his imprisonment.

Because the Wallabout ships were intended for privateers (among others) and Sag Harbor was a sea-faring town that contributed many to the Revolution, it is not surprising that multiple residents, including **David Hand** and **Nathan Fordham**, brother of Frederic, experienced the hellish conditions on these infamous prison ships.

References : **The Prison Ships**
Lihistory.com, John Burke e-mail, John Hayes e-mail.
Armbruster, Eugene. Wallabout Bay Prison Ships 1776-1783. NY : 1920.
Thompson, Benjamin. The History of Long Island. New York : 1839.
A. Meyer

SAG HARBOR'S
REVOLUTIONARY WAR PATRIOTS
Buried in Sag Harbor's Old Burying Ground

Captain Lester Beebe
Stone # 76a

Captain Lester Beebe, son of Samuel Beebe, was born June 12, 1754. He married Bethiah Brown in Sag Harbor, New York, April 1, 1776. She was born at Orient, New York, on June 12, 1759, the daughter of Benjamin Brown.

Lester Beebe served in the military in Southold, New York, during the Revolutionary War. Frederic Mather in his book, *The Refugees of 1776 from L. I. to Connecticut,* states that, "Beebe, Lester 6, Captain (Samuel 5,4,3,2, John 1) from Southold. On January 11, 1783 he was permitted to go to L.I. and bring off money & c. for his family." He was captured by the enemy, but paid for his liberty. After the War he removed to Sag Harbor, and later, in company with Henry Ekford, became a noted ship builder in New York City. He lived in Flushing for several years.

In 1820, while living in Sag Harbor, Lester Beebe hired Samuel Schellinger, a millwright from Amagansett, and his apprentice, Pardon Tabor, to build a windmill. The mill stood on Suffolk Street, Sag Harbor, on property at the rear of John Sherry's. In operation during Sag Harbor's spectacular whaling industry, it became known as the "Flag on the Mill, Ship in the Bay" windmill, as a flag was flown from a pole at the top of the mill when a ship was sighted in the bay returning from a whaling voyage. After Lester Beebe's death, his son, Jason Beebe put the mill up for sale in 1835. Moved several times, the windmill stands today on the Berwind estate, Ocean Road, Bridgehampton, New York.

Children born to Captain Lester Beebe and his wife, Bethiah were :
1. Infant Beebe, born at Sag Harbor January 9, 1777, died January 17, 1777.
2. Lester Beebe, born at Sag Harbor May 10, 1778, died in 1797 at age 19.
3. Polly Beebe, born at Sag Harbor July 18, 1780, died in 1807 at age 26.

4. Eliphalet Beebe, born at Sag Harbor September 8, 1782, died July 1783.
5. James Beebe, born at Sag Harbor September 8, 1784, died in 1801. He went to sea and never returned. He was 17 years old.
6. Jason Beebe, born at Sag Harbor June 7, 1787, died September 2, 1835, at the age of forty-eight. His gravestone reads died September 4, 1835.
7. Thomas Beebe, born at Sag Harbor July 11, 1793, died in 1807 at age 13.

Sadly, four of the Beebe children died before reaching adulthood. Captain Lester Beebe died at Sag Harbor November 4, 1852 at the age of seventy-eight. (His grave stone in the Old Burying Ground gives his date of death as November 11, 1852). Bethiah Beebe died February 17, 1823 at the age of sixty-three and is also buried in the Old Burying Ground.

References : **Captain Lester Beebe**
Beebe Family Records owned in 1948 by William T. Beebe of Sag Harbor. Article reproduced on Broderbund Softwares Family Archives CD #173 (Genealogies of L.I. Families,1600-1800).
DAR Patriot Index (Washington, DC)
Mather, Frederic. The Refugees of 1776 from L.I. to Connecticut. 3rd ed. Baltimore : Clearfield Publishing Co., 1995. hereafter cited as Mather, *Rufugees.*
OBG inventories of William Wallace Tooker 1885, Louis Tooker Vail, 1950 and OBG Committee, 2001.

Captain Aaron Clark
Stone # 12

Captain Aaron Clark was born in Connecticut to Abraham Clark and Sarah Hetfield, on September 13, 1758. When Aaron was seventeen years old he joined the Fourth Regiment of the Orange County, New York, Militia, and served in the Revolutionary War.

Aaron Clark married Huldah _____, who was born in 1767 and died January 26, 1837. At least four children were born to them all of whom met untimely deaths while living in Sag Harbor.

1. Aaron Clark, born in 1797, died November 5, 1800, age 2.

2. Daughter, born about 1798, died October 4, 1800, age 2.
3. Huldah Clark, born 1798 and died September 12, 1813, age 15.
4. Daughter born in 1805 and died November 1, 1805, age seven months.
5. Child born in 1811 and died September 12, 1813, age two, of dysentery.

Aaron Clark died in Sag Harbor on June 11, 1855, at the age of ninety-eight, and is buried in the Old Burying Ground.

References : **Aaron Clark**
Mather, *Refugees.*
OBG inventories of William Wallace Tooker 1885, Louis Tooker Vail 1950 and OBG Committee 2001.
Sag Harbor Presbyterian Church record book of baptisms, marriages and deaths, hereafter cited as Presbyterian Church records.

Braddock Corey
Stone # 236

Braddock Corey was the son of Abraham Corey of Sag Harbor, and Alece Braddick. He was born at North Haven, a community north of Sag Harbor in January 1735. Braddock Corey became a property owner and man of influence in the village. He married Charity Fordham, daughter of Nathan Fordham and Abigail Bowdich about 1765. Charity was born in 1742.

During the Revolutionary War Braddock Corey helped take refugees to Connecticut to escape British control of Long Island. According to Frederic G. Mather in his book, *The Refugees of 1776 from Long Island to Connecticut,* Braddock Corey landed at Chester with a load of two hogshead of wheat and six sheep, and at East Haddam with four hogshead of wheat, three loads of goods and forty-four passengers.

Braddock Corey was a carpenter and craftsman by trade, but supplemented his income by his job as a butcher. In 1788 he donated a lot on the corner of Madison and Jefferson Streets on which Sag Harbor's first public school was built. Braddock Corey was also involved in law enforcement in the growing port of Sag Harbor, and was given the job of punishing a thief by inflicting thirty lashes upon him.

Braddock Corey died at Sag Harbor on February 1, 1809 at the age of seventy-four. He and his wife, Charity, whose untimely death occurred February 12, 1775, when she was only thirty-three, are buried in the Old Burying Ground.

References : **Braddock Corey**
Mather. *Refugees.*
Zaykowski, Dorothy Ingersoll. *Sag Harbor; the Story of an American Beauty.* Mattituck, NY : Amereon, Ltd., 1991.
OBG inventories of William Wallace Tooker 1885, Louis Tooker Vail 1950 and OBG Committee 2001.

Captain Daniel Fordham
Stone # 203

Daniel Fordham, son of Nathan Fordham and Abigail Bowditch, was born at Mecox, Bridgehampton, New York, December 6, 1730. During the Revolutionary War, Daniel, two of his sons, and his brother, were all involved.

Daniel and his brother, Esquire Nathan, were two of the early settlers of Sag Harbor, both having lived there from at least 1769. Daniel married Phebe Jessup on Hog Neck (North Haven), just north of Sag Harbor, on November 11, 1756. Phebe was the daughter of Nathaniel Jessup and Phebe Havens, and was born in Noyack March 3, 1736.

Daniel and Phebe were the parents of ten children.

1. Nathan Fordham (Captain) born August 7, 1757, died January 7, 1838, age 80.
2. An unnamed child, born and died in August 1759.
3. Frances Fordham, born December 4, 1761, married Josiah Winslow Wentworth, died June 22, 1835, age 75.
4. Charlotte Fordham, born March 7, 1763, died June 1, 1813, age 50.
5. Frederic Fordham, born March 27, 1765, died June 25, 1782, age 18.
6. Jarius Fordham, born August 2, 1767, died July 24, 1831, age 63.

7. Thaddeus Fordham, born July 29, 1769, died March
   28, 1843, age 73.
8. Samuel Fordham, born November 14, 1771, died
   February 27, 1803, age 31.
9. Joel Fordham, born April 4, 1774.
10. Daniel Fordham, born June 2, 1779, died in 1806,
   age 27. Lost at sea in possible hurricane.

Daniel Fordham served in the military on Long Island about
1776. He was an Ensign in the 8th Company of Colonel Mulford's
Regiment of Minute Men, and took part in the Battle of Long Island.
He was a refugee to Saybrook, Connecticut, and he signed the
Association in 1775.

Daniel Fordham was a mariner and also an inn keeper in Sag
Harbor after the Revolution. His wife, Phebe died November 4, 1806,
at the age of 70, and Daniel died June 12, 1816, at the age of 86. They
are buried in the Old Burying Ground.

References : **Daniel Fordham**
Hedges, Hon. H.P.. *Early Sag Harbor, An Address Before the Sag Harbor
Historical Society, February 4, 1896.* Sag Harbor, NY : H. Hunt,
printer. 1902.
Mather, *Refugees.*
Sleight, Harry D.. *Sag Harbor in Earlier Days.* Bridgehampton, NY:
Hampton Press, 1930.
OBG inventories of William Wallace Tooker 1885, Louis Tooker Vail
1950 and OBG Committee 2001.
Vail, *Fordham Genealogy,* unpublished manuscript.

Captain Nathan Fordham, Esquire
Stone # 244

Nathan Fordham, older brother of Captian Daniel Fordham,
and son of Nathan Fordham and Abigail Bowditch, was born April 2,
1722, probably in Mecox, Bridgehampton, New York. He lived his
early years on Shelter Island, and on April 14, 1752 married Abigail
Havens. Children born to Nathan and Abigail were :

1. Mary Fordham, born November 25, 1752.
2. John Nathan Fordham, born July 11, 1754.

During the Revolutionary War, Captain Nathan Fordham transported Refugees from Long Island to Connectiuct. His own family was moved by Captain Zebulon Cooper from Sag Harbor to Saybrook, Connecticut. He also served on a committee of Safety and on a sub-committee relative to cannon and ammunition in 1775. He signed the Association in 1775. Frederick Mather, in his *Refugees,* states that Nathan Fordham was plundered by Lieutenant Jacob White and Samuel Combs. He petitioned the General Assembly of Connecticut for relief which was granted in May 1778. From East Haddam, Connecticut oon July 27, 1779, he petitioned the Governor and Council of Connecticut for permission to go to Long Island for salt, from his estate. On March 20, 1780, he, with others, was allowed to go for salt and supplies. On October 11, 1782 he was permitted to return to Long Island with his family and effects.

Captain Nathan Fordham's wife, Abigail, died September 15, 1796, and is buried in the Old Burying Ground. Three years later, on November 13, 1799, Nathan Fordham married again. Widow Sarah Reeves, his second wife, was 64 years old and Nathan, 77, when they wed. Sarah died November 12, 1805, at the age of 70, and Nathan died November 13, 1805, just one day later at the age of 83. Nathan and Sarah are buried together in the same grave in the Old Burying Ground.

References: **Captain Nathan Fordham, Esquire**
Mather, *Refugees.*
OBG inventories of William Wallace Tooker 1885, Louis Tooker Vail 1950 and OBG Committee 2001.
Vail. *Fordham Genealogy.*

<h2 style="text-align:center">Frederic Fordham
Stone # 200</h2>

Frederic Fordham, fourth child and second son of Captain Daniel Fordham and his wife, Phebe Jessup, was born at Sag Harbor, on March 27, 1765. Although only sixteen, he followed his father, brother and uncle to fight for his country's freedom.

Frederic was captured and confined to one of the Prison Ships in the Wallabout, New York Harbor, where he suffered many hardships and privations. Frederic was released, but died shortly thereafter, on June 25, 1782, due to the treatment he received while imprisoned. He is buried in the Old Burying Ground.

References : **Frederic Fordham**
OBG inventories of William Wallace Tooker 1885, Luois Tooker Vail 1950 and OBG Committee 2001.
Vail. *Fordham Genealogy.*

John Nathan Fordham
Stone # 279

John Nathan Fordham, son of Nathan Fordham, Esquire, and Abigail Havens, was born July 11, 1754. He married his first wife, Jane Foster on May 17, 1775 and immediately left for battle. Jane was born in 1760 and died April 6, 1799 while giving birth to their tenth child. He signed the Association that same year, and was a Refugee to East Haddam, Connecticut. John Nathan Fordham served under Colonel Philip Van Courtlandt in the New York 2nd Regiment, and as a Sergeant Major under Colonel Lewis Dubuis in the New York 5th Regiment.

John Natham Fordham and Jane Foster Fordham's children were :

1. Peletiah, born September 17, 1776 at Saybrook, Connecticut and died Octover 1, 1776.
2. Peletiah, born September 3, 1778 at East Haddam, Connecticut, and died in October 1778.
3. Mary, born May 27, 1781 at East Haddam, Connecticut, and died July 1, 1807, age 26.
4. Roxana, born February 7, 1785 at Sag Harbor, and died July 10, 1804, age 19, in childbirth.
5. Peletiah, born July 6, 1787, died December 19, 1858.
6. Sibyl Foster, born April 7, 1790.
7. Charity, born December 7, 1792, died January 1817.
8. Julia Ann, born October 2, 1795, died December 2, 1821.
9. John Nathan, born February 18, 1798, died October 7, 1798.
10. Jane Maria, born March 1799, died April 6, 1799. Buried next to her mother.

John Nathan Fordham was married again to Charity Halsey, daughter of Charity White and Jesse Halsey. Charity, born November 18, 1763, became John Nathan's second wife in 1799. They were the parents of four children :

1. John Nathan, born October 12, 1800, died June 8, 1816, age 15.
2. Nathan Y., born September 21, 1802, died February 17, 1880.
3. Charles Halsey Mortimer, born April 7, 1804, died December 24 or 29, 1843.
4. Roxana Stewart, born September 1, 1805, died March 7, 1890.

John Nathan Fordham died March 1, 1808, and his wife, Charity, being filled with grief, took her own life, June 17, 1810. John Nathan and Charity are buried in the Old Burying Ground.

References : **John Nathan Fordham**
OBG inventories of William Wallace Tooker 1885, Louis Tooker Vail 1950 and OBG Committee 2001.
Vail. *Fordham Genealogy.*

Nathan Fordham, son of Daniel and Phebe
(buried in the OBG and later moved to Oakland Cemetery)

Nathan Fordham, son of Captain Daniel and Phebe Jessup Fordham, was born in Sag Harbor, August 7, 1757. He was the older brother of Frederic Fordham, and like his brother was captured and spent time on a Prison Ship. Unlike Frederic, Nathan survived the ordeal and lived to an advanced age.

Nathan Fordham married Mary Howell, daughter of James Howell and Lucretia Havens, on July 29, 1783. Mary was born at Sag Harbor on January 7, 1762.

In 1776 Nathan Fordham was captain of a ship that transported Patriots from Sag Harbor to Connecticut. He brought to Rope Ferry, part of the effects of John Hudson. He enlisted at Sag Harbor and served under Captain John Davis and Colonel Henry B. Livingston. Nathan Fordham and his family were Refugees to East Haddam in 1776.

Following the war, Nathan was master of the sloop, *Polly*, in 1792, a ship that carried goods and passengers between Sag Harbor and Albany. He also was Captain of the sloop, *Favorite*, which sailed between Sag Harbor and New York.

Nathan Fordham died at Sag Harbor on January 7, 1838, at the age of eighty-one. His wife, Mary, died at Sag Harbor November 2, 1818 at the age of fifty-six. Both were buried in the Old Burying Ground, but when Madison Street was widened, they, along with many other individuals were re-interred in the newly opened Oakland Cemetery on Jermain Avenue, Sag Harbor.

References : **Nathan Fordham, son of Daniel and Phebe Mather,** *Refugees.*
Vail. *Fordham Genealogy*
OBG inventories of William Wallace Tooker   1885, Louis Tooker
Vail 1950 and OBG Committee 2001.
List of individuals removed to Oakland Cemetery.

Hugh Gelston
Stone # 259

Hugh Gelston, son of Maltby and Mary Gelston, was born November 19, 1754, in Bridgehampton, Long Island, New York. He grew up in the family home on Butter Lane. Hugh was the brother of David Gelston, Collector of the Port of Sag Harbor from 1801-1820.

Hugh Gelston served in the Suffolk County Militia's 1st Regiment of Minute Men. Gelston and Henry P. Dering were a committee of two who notified Brig. General Rose that the British fleet was in Gardiner's Bay and that Sag Harbor was no longer safe. Hugh Gelston and his wife, Puah, were refugees to East Haddam, Connecticut, having fled there to escape the British occupation of Long Island and to fight for freedom. Puah was the daughter of David Corwith of Bridgehampton.

In November 1779 he petitioned to winter his horses on Long Island, and in December of that year, he was allowed to go to Long Island for 300 bushels of salt.

When Hugh and Puah returned to Long Island after the war, they moved to Sag Harbor, and lived the rest of their lives there. They died without issue, Hugh on April 26, 1828, and Puah on August 27, 1829, and both are buried in the Old Burying Ground.

References : **Hugh Gelston**
Hoff. *Genealogies of Long Island Families.* Genealogical Publishing Co., Inc. 1987.
Mather, *Refugees.*

OBG inventories of William Wallace Tooker 1885, Louis Tooker Vail 1950 and OBG Committee 2001

Josiah Hand
Stone # 185

Josiah Hand, son of David Hand and Zerviah Stuart, was born October 31, 1756, at Sagaponack, Long Island, New York. Josiah's father and six brothers were all involved in the American Revolution.

At the age of nineteen Josiah served in Colonel Smith's Regiment of Minute Men. His military career spanned throughout the war. He was at the Battle of Long Island and with George Washington at the Battle of Trenton.

Josiah Hand married twice. His first wife, Hannah Mulford died in 1799, and on December 15, 1800 he married Susannah Gardiner. He was the father of six children.

In 1796 Josiah Hand was a trustee of the Brick Kiln School, where his children Zeruviah, Jane, Fanny and Mary, were students. The family lived at Brick Kiln, between Sag Harbor and Bridgehampton, and Josiah Hand died there December 12, 1835, at the age of seventy-nine. He is buried in the Old Burying Ground.

References : **Josiah Hand**
Mather, *Refugees.*
Rattray, Jeannette Edwards. *East Hampton History.* Garden City, NY : Country Life Press, 1953.
OBG inventories of William Wallace Tooker 1885, Louis Tooker Vail 1950 and OBG Committee 2001.

Captain William Havens
Stone # 198

Born at Shelter Island, New York, in 1747, William Havens was the son of William Havens and Ruth Falconer. William married his first wife, Desire, in 1770, and then Bethiah Bowditch (his second cousin) about 1775. Bethiah was the daughter of Joel Bowditch and Bethiah Case of Shelter Island. Children of William and Bethiah were :

1. Mary Havens, born about 1777
2. Hamutal Havens, born about 1777 or 78

3. Lucretia Havens, born about 1779.

During the Revolutionary War, Captain Havens acted for Colonel Henry B. Livingston, in securing vessels to sail refugees to Connecticut. He served in the 2nd, 3rd, and 4th of the Line, the last two as Lieutenant. William Havens and his family fled to Connecticut where he continued to serve. William Havens became a Privateer, commanding the ships, *Beaver, Jay,* and *Retaliation.*

William Havens drowned at Cape Cod, Massachusetts on November 21, 1798, and was brought to Sag Harbor for burial in the Old Burying Ground.

References : **William Havens**
Havens, Barrington S., *The Havens Family in Suffolk County, New York*
Mather. *Refugees.*
OBG List of Louis Tooker Vail, 1950
OBG inventories of William Wallace Tooker 1885, Louis Tooker Vail 1950 and OBG Committee 2001.

Captain William Havens, stone # 198

Captain William Parker
Stone # 163

William Parker was born about 1754, the son of _____.
About the time of the American Revolution he married Aseneth
_____, who was born about 1752. Children of William and Aseneth
Parker were :

1. Henry Parker (Captain) born 1777, died October 31, 1840.
2. William Parker, Jr., born 1779.
3. Gilbert Parker, born 1782, drowned off Sandy Hook
   November 11, 1804, age 22.
4. Son, born 1792, and who drowned July 20, 1796, age 4.
5. Nancy Maria Parker, born 1806, died October 12, 1828, age
   22.

William Parker and his family were one of the founding families
of Sag Harbor. In 1808 he was the master of the Sag Harbor built
schooner, *Willing Maid.*
   William Parker, Jr. married Mary Fordham in Sag Harbor,
August 26, 1800. Mary was born in East Haddam, Connecticut on
May 27, 1781. She was the daughter of refugee John Nathan
Fordham and his wife Jane. Mary and William Jr. were the parents of :

1. George Parker, born 1802, and died November 28, 1822,
   age 20.
2. Mary or Maria Parker, born 1804, and who married William
   J. Furman, a New York merchant, and died at the age of 17.

Captain William Parker died October 3, 1832 at the age of
seventy-eight, and is buried in the Old Burying Ground.

References : **Captain William Parker**
OBG List of William Wallace Tooker, 1885.
Mather. *Refugees.*
Sleight, Harry D.. *Sag Harbor in Earlier Days.* Bridgehampton,
NY: Hampton Press, 1930.
Presbyterian Church records

Dr. Jeremiah Hedges
Stone # 226

Dr. Jeremiah Hedges was the son of Timothy Hedges of East Hampton, Long Island, New York, and born about 1746. Jeremiah married Ruth Norris, daughter of John Norris of Bridgehampton, Long Island, New York about 1762. Their only child, a son, Jeremiah W. Hedges was born March 19, 1763.

Dr. Jeremiah Hedges was a graduate of Yale. He took an oath of allegiance in East Hampton, and during the Revolutionary War served as a surgeon. He died August 17, 1797 at the age of fifty one, and is buried in the Old Burying Ground.

References : **Dr. Jeremiah Hedges**
Rattray. Jeannette Edwards. *East Hampton History.*
Vail, *Fordam Genealogy.*
OBG inventories of William Wallace Tooker 1885, Louis Tooker Vail 1950 and OBG Committee 2001.
Presbyterian Church records

Captain Benjamin Price
Stone # 13

Benjamin Price was born about 1738. He married Jemima _____, who was one of the first members of the Sag Harbor Presbyterian Church. Prior to the Revolution, Benjamin Price and his family lived on North Haven, a small community just over the bridge from Sag Harbor.

In June 1775, when in his thirties, Benjamin Price served in the Revolutionary War under Colonel James Clinton in New York's 3rd Regiment. In September 1776, Price, his wife and three young daughters were taken to Stonington, Connecticut by Captain David Sayre. The family remained in Connecticut at least through 1783, before returning to Long Island.

Along with his three daughters, a fourth girl, Jemima, was born in Connecticut and baptised April 20, 1783, at the Rocky Hill Church. When the family returned to Sag Harbor they lived near the Methodist Church.

Benjamin Price's wife, Jemima, died June 10, 1817 at the age of sixty nine, and Benjamin died a year later on December 8, 1818, at the age of eighty. Both are interred in the Old Burying Ground.

References : **Benjamin Price**
Sleight, Harry D., *Sag Harbor in Earlier Days.*
OBG inventories of William Wallace Tooker 1885, Louis Tooker Vail
1950 and OBG Committee 2001.
Presbyterian Church records.

John Squire
Stone # 7

Born in 1739, **John Squire** was the son of John Squire and Phebe Baker. About 1775 he married Margery (or Hannah) Cable, daughter of George Cable and Sarah Shaw.

John Squire served in Captain Elias Hand's Company from Bridgehampton, Long Island, New York. Mather, in his book, *The Refugees of 1776 from Long Island to Connecticut,* states that John Squire probably served in Connecticut and may have been the one who was appointed Comm'y in Fairfield, April 1780.

When John Squire died on June 2, 1807, his obituary in the June 8, 1807 Suffolk County Gazette, printed at Sag Harbor read :

'The duties of his noble station were performed with a punctuality and faithfulness seldom to be found. Every day of his life he has been devoted to some useful employment either for himself or in the service of his neighbors. He obeyed to the fullest in part that sublime moral maxim of the Gospel. He had not an enemy in the world and bore no enmity to anything but vice and idleness. A faithful husband and friend, a wife who from indispositions of both body and mind required every day their long connection the patient exercise of all those virtues which try the faithful husband and affectionate friend. Everyone knew him and knew where to find him."

References : **John Squire**
Mather. *Refugees.*
Suffolk County Gazette, June 8, 1807.
OBG inventories of William Wallace Tooker 1885, Louis Tooker Vail 1950 and OBG Committee 2001.

Captain Peleg Niles
Stone # 23

Captain Peleg Niles was born in 1758. About 1781 he married Phebe _____. They were the parents of lt least three children:

1. Phebe Niles, born 1786, died October 23, 1804, age 17.
2. George Niles, born January 20, 1787.
2. Ephraim Niles, born August 7, 1791, died October 7, 1823.

Peleg Niles and his wife, Phebe, joined the Presbyterian Church at Sag Harbor September 5, 1800.

During the Revolutionary War, Peleg Niles was captain of the ship, *Spy*, a privateer that cruised between Stamford and Nantucket.

Peleg Niles died at age sixty-three, September 27, 1828, of jaundice, and his wife, Phebe, died May 11, 1829, at the age of seventy-two. Both are interred in the Old Burying Ground.

References: **Peleg Niles**
OBG inventories of William Wallace Tooker 1885., Louis Tooker Vail 1950 and OBG Committee 2001.
Presbyterian Church records.

Captain Luther Hildreth
Stone # 221

Born in 1757, **Luther Hildreth** enlisted at the age of nineteen from Bridgehampton, Long Island, New York. He served in Captain David Pierson's Company of Minute Men, and Josiah Smith's Regiment of Minute Men. He signed the Articles of Association in 1775. Luther Hildreth married Mehitabel _____, who was born in 1759 and died July 31, 1791, at the age of thirty-two. Luther and Mehitabel were the parents of Mary, born in 1788 and died June 3, 1789, at the age of one.

Luther Hildreth married a second time, to Abigail _____, born in 1763 and died April 20, 1836, at the age of seventy-three. An infant son of Luther and Abigail died March 6, 1793. Abigail was a member of the Sag Harbor Presbyterian Church, having joined in1791.

Captain Luther Hildreth died December 11, 1826, at the age of sixty-nine, and is buried with his two wives in the Old Burying Ground.

References : **Captain Luther Hildreth**
Mather, *Refugees.*
OBG inventories of William Wallace Tooker 1885, Louis Tooker Vail 1950 and OBG Commitee 2001.
Presbyterian Church records.

Ephraim L' Hommedieu
Stone # 44

Ephraim L'Hommedieu was born in 1755, a member of a French Hugenot family that came to Sag Harbor in early times. He enlisted in the Revolutionary War and served in Captain Zephaniah Rogers 1st Company, and in Joseph Smith's Regiment of Minute Men. This company was formed for the protection of the inhabitants and stock of Long Island.

Following the end of the war Ephriam L'Hommedieu married Mehitable _____. He died at the young age of forty on May 30, 1795. Mehitable died on October 19, 1815. Both are buried in the Old Burying Ground.

References : **Ephraim L'Hommedieu**
Adams, John Truslow. *The History of the Town of Southampton.* Bridgehampton, NY : Hampton Press, 1918.
Geneva White Baird. *DAR Gravestone Inscriptions,* 1930's.
OBG inventories of William Wallace Tooker 1885, Louis Tooker Vail 1950 and OBG Committee 2001.

Stephen Jessup
Stone # 92

Born about 1758, **Stephen Jessup** took an oath of allegiance in May 1775 at the age of seventeen, and signed the Articles of Association. Stephen Jessup married Vica _____, who was born in 1759 and died August 27, 1830 at the age of seventy-one. Stephen died November 29, 1833 at the age of seventy-four. (Presbyterian Church records state that he died November 21st and that he died of a fit.) Stephen Jessup was laid to rest in the Old Burying Ground.

References : **Stephen Jessup**
OBG inventories of William Wallace Tooker 1885, Louis Tooker Vail
1950 and OBG Committee 2001.

David Tarbell
Stone # 78

David Tarbell, born in 1745, served in the military of the
Revolutionary War in Suffolk County June 1776. He was an ensign in
the 1st Regiment of Minute Men, Captain David Pierson's company.
David Tarbell married Phebe _____, who was born in
1746 and died July 10, 1829 at the age of eighty-three. David Tarbell
died December 24, 1833 at the age of eighty-eight and is buried in the
Old Burying Ground.

References : **David Tarbell**
OBG inventories of William Wallace Tooker 1885, Louis Tooker Vail
1950 and OBG Committee 2001.
Presbyterian Church records.

Captain Clark Truman
Stone # 38

Clark Truman was born in New London, Connecticut, on
September 26, 1736, the son of Eleazer Truman and Mary Clark. He
came to Long Island to live, took the oath of allegiance and signed the
Articles of Association in 1775. In 1776 he brought William Deval
(Duvall) and his grain from Long Island to East Haddam.
Clark Truman died October 2, 1795 and is buried in the Old
Burying Ground. (There are two broken bases next to Clark Truman's
gravestone which may have belonged to members of his family.)

References : **Clark Truman**
OBG inventories of William Wallace Tooker 1885, Louis Tooker Vail
1950 and OBG Committee 2001.
Presbyterian Church records.

Silas Stuart
Stone # 193

Silas Stuart was born in 1743 and lived at the Brick Kilns, between Sag Harbor and Bridgehampton, Long Island, New York. He enlisted at Bridgehampton in 1775, and served in the 3rd and 4th Orange Regiments. He was a refugee to Connecticut, being taken there by Captain David Sayre. While there he served in the Connecticut Line.

In 1762, when Silas Stuart was just nineteen, he married Abigail _____ who was born in 1740. They had at least two children.

1. Silas Stuart, Jr., born in 1769.
2. Austin Stuart, born in 1770, and died September 2, 1798 at the age of twenty-eight.

Silas Stuart, Jr. married Mary (Polly) _____ October 1, 1799. Polly died March 7, 1801, and in 1803 he married Temperance Parsons. They were parents of two children who died as infants, one March 4, 1804 and the other February 6, 1812.

Silas Stuart, Sr. died November 16, 1800 at the age of fifty-seven and his wife, Abigail on July 16, 1816 at the age of seventy-six. All are buried in the Old Burying Ground.

References : **Silas Stuart**
Mather. *Refugees*
Baird, Geneva White. *DAR Tombstone Inscriptions.*
OBG inventories of William Wallace Tooker 1885, Louis Tooker Vail 1950 and OBG Committee 2001.
Presbyterian Church records.

Caleb Cooper
(buried in the Old Burying Ground and later moved to Oakland Cemetery)

Caleb Cooper, born in 1745, was the youngest son of Thomas and Mary Cooper, and lived his early years in Southampton, Long Island, New York. He married Abigail _____ about 1772 and had the following children, William, Caleb and Huntting.

Caleb Cooper was a Revolutionary War patriot, having taken the oath in May 1775.

Following the war the Southampton Town Trustees, in 1789, recommended the Commissioner of Highways go to Sag Harbor with Caleb Cooper and Jonathan Rogers to lay out a road from Main Street to the Old Wharf. This road was called Cooper Street.

In 1795 Caleb Cooper was a Trustee in the early Southampton schoolhouse.

Abigail Cooper died May 13, 1840 and Caleb died July 19, 1834. The *Sag Harbor Corrector* notes his death at the age of eighty-nine and describes him as "an old and respectable citizen." The remains of Caleb Cooper were removed from the Old Burying Ground and taken to Oakland Cemetery in 1860.

References : Caleb Cooper
Howell, George Rogers. *The Early History of Southampton, Long Island, New York.* New York : J.N. Hallock, publisher, 1866.
Mather. *Refugees.*
Zaykowski, Dorothy Ingersoll. *Sag Harbor; the Story of an American Beauty.* Mattituck : Amereon, Ltd., 1991.
The Sag Harbor Corrector, July 19, 1834.
OBG Inventories of William Wallace Tooker 1885, Louis Tooker Vail 1950, OBG Committee 2001.

B. Schwartz and D. Zaykowski

Nancy Beebe, stone # 71
Weeping Willow and Urn motif

THE OLD BURYING GROUND'S SEGREGATED SOUTH-EAST END

While working and researching the south-east or Latham Street side of the Old Burying Ground, some interesting facts were discovered. First, it appears that all of the local African American residents were buried there; second, that all of the Portuguese sailors were buried there; and third, there seems to be a great deal of unused burial space at that end of the cemetery. It means that segregation was obviously practiced in Sag Harbor's Old Burying Ground when it came to burying its minority residents. It also means that much of what appears to be the unused space is in all likelihood filled with Sag Harbor's early African American population who died and were buried there in unmarked graves.

Before St. David A.M.E. Zion Cemetery and Oakland Cemetery opened in 1840, the Old Burying Ground was the only public graveyard in the village. In addition to the African Americans who are buried there in marked graves, there were at least seventeen other documented deaths of black residents in Sag Harbor between 1798 and 1832. These seventeen are listed in a record book of marriages, baptisms and deaths in the Sag Harbor Presbyterian Church archives. They are :

> **Robert**, a Negro, died March 16, 1798, age 24.
> James Mitchell's negro, died August 11, 1798, age 28.
> **Cyrus**, a man of color, died November 2, 1798, age 45.
> Peleg Latham's Negro lad, died June 16, 1801, age 19.
> **Simmony**, Esquire Fordham's Negro woman, died September 12, 1805, age 55.
> **Black Biny's** child, died September 18, 1813.
> **Dutchess**, a woman of color, died March 26, 1815, age 49.
> Mr. Mitchell's black boy, died April 22, 1816, age 2.
> **Marvin**, a man of color, died December 6, 1817, age 46.
> Infant black child, died November 3, 1821, age 8 months.
> **Peggy Hedges**, a woman of color, died November 16, 1826, age 83.

Dick, a man of color, died May 1, 1828, age 53.
Mary Nicoll, a woman of color, died September 18, 1828, age 49.
Temperance Prince, a woman of color, died January 9,1829, age 58.
Caroline Gelston, a woman of color, died March 22, 1830, age 45.
Maria, a woman of color, died June 16, 1832, age 58.

If these individuals were buried in Sag Harbor, they were buried in the Old Burying Ground in unmarked graves, and most likely, there were even more who died prior to the church's record keeping.

Seven African American residents are buried at the southeast end of the cemetery with grave stones marking their burial places:

#115 **Judith Jack** (a colored woman) born in 1753 and died April 7, 1828, at the age of 75. The Presbyterian Church records have the date of her death as April 18th. The were many members of the Jack family living in this area, among them, Abraham, Catherine, Dinah, Nathaniel, Benjamin and Jason. They lived in East Hampton, Montauk, Bridgehampton and Sag Harbor. Jason Jack was a whaler who sailed out of Cold Spring Harbor on the whale ship, *Tuscarora*, in 1842.

#116 **Brewster Miller** (or as his death notice in the *Sag Harbor Corrector*, reads, "Brister" Miller, colored man). Brewster Miller, who died on January 28, 1846, at the age of 75 was a highly respected citizen of Sag Harbor. It was unusual to have any sort of a tribute or obituary published unless the deceased was an important person. Brewster Miller had the distinction of being remembered with the following tribute:

"Brister filled his station in life with honesty and propriety, was peaceable and content with his situation, and his account current, and will give the Recording Angel but little difficulty to settle."

His grave stone is inscribed, "The Noblest Work of God; An Honest Man."

#117 **Tamos Tucker**, whose stone is next to Brewster Miller, was born in 1772 and died November 13, 1838 at the age of 66. The unusual spelling of his first name may be a variation of Thomas, or it may be that he was named after a member of the Tamus family who lived in Sag Harbor.

Brewster Miller, stone # 116

#121 is a person known only as **"Robin"** in earlier inventories done at the Old Burying Ground. The church records list a **"Robert"** having died the same date and the same age. The grave stone is broken and much of it is missing, with only the date and his age left to identify it as Robin/Robert's grave. His stone was said to originally have read, "Robin (or Robert), a Negro, died March 16, 1798, age 24."

#122 **Caroline Prince,** wife of Simeon Prince, was born in 1789 and died March 12, 1830, at the age of 41. Caroline's husband, Simeon, may have been a member of the Prince family who were slaves belonging to Nathaniel Sylvester of Shelter Island. The record book also lists Temperance, wife of Thomas Prince colored, as having died January 9,1829. Perhaps Caroline's husband and the other Prince family members are buried in unmarked graves in the Old Burying Ground.

#131 **Mary Bird,** born in 1830, was the eleven year old daughter of John and Rachel Bird, who died February 7, 1841. No other members of the Bird family are buried in the Old Burying Ground that we know of. The Church records note that John Bird married Rachel Shrew on January 13, 1826, and that they were "people of color." John Bird apparently died young as a Widow Bird married another identified only as "Frank" in May of 1833.

#135 and 136 are **Mehetabel Solomon** and her daughter, **Elizabeth Solomon** who are buried next to each other. Mehetabel, wife of Samuel Solomon, died June 25, 1828, at the age of 46. Elizabeth, daughter of Mehetabel and Samuel Solomon, died December 21, 1819, at the age of 15. Samuel is recorded as an "old colored man" having died in 1854. Samuel married a second time, as Hannah Solomon, wife of Samuel, joined the Presbyterian Church in 1829 and died in 1858. It isn't known where Samuel and Hannah are buried, but they may lie in unmarked graves in the Old Burying Ground.

In addition to the African Americans buried at the south-east end of the burying ground, there are graves of five Portuguese men and one Portuguese child. During Sag Harbor's whaling days, ships returning home often arrived with crew members they took on in foreign ports. Most of them were from Fayal and the Portuguese Azores. All five of the men were involved in the whale fishery and died in the 1830's.

Portuguese sailors were considered good whalemen who performed their duties with skill and diligence. When in port they were often seen walking the streets of Sag Harbor selling scrimshaw and shellcraft made while they were at sea.

Another Portuguese sailor was interred in the Old Burying Ground behind the Arsenal that stood on Union Street on the site of the present Meigs monument. That man was Favieco Maeceia, aged 44. His remains were re-interred in Oakland Cemetery. An epitaph on his stone reads;

"Tho Boreas' winds and Neptune's waves
have tossed me to and fro,
By God's decree, you plainly see,
I'm harbored here below."

Buried in the same plot as Favieco Maeceia are the wives of Antone Silvia and Emanuel Olives. These men married DeCastro girls of Sag Harbor. Jospeh Enos was another Portuguese who came to Sag Harbor and remained here. In 1873 he purchased the old schoolhouse that stood on the corner of Madison and Jefferson Streets, moved it to Glover Street, and converted it into a house. Joseph Enos sailed aboard the whaleship, *Susan*, in 1863. Others of the Enos family lived here as well. Abraham Enos served in the Civil War, and Charles Enos married Maggie Gibbon in Sag Harbor in1880.

The following Portuguese are in the Old Burying Ground with stones marking their burial places. The inscriptions are quite illegible and the words are as we interpreted them after much study.

#128 **Francisco Lucianni**, died 18 June (illegible).

#127 **Joachim Joze Panna,** (illegible) Sua Mai Escolasica Marianna Panna, 21 annos 17 July (illegible).

#126 **Francisco Joze Goncalues Labanja,** Filbe de Luis Joze-Goncalues Labanja, Sua Mai Escolalica Marianna, Moroua 12 de Ominbro com 21 annos.

#125 **Esther I.**, daughter of Francisco Ignaios and Jennet M.Demilo died April 23, 1845, age 2 months.

#123 **Juan Antonio Dalosta**, son of Antonio and Maria Luiza Dalosta, died May 28, 1845, age 20.

#129 **Manuel Francisco**, (illegible) fell from the foremast of the ship, *Hannibal*, on June 24, 1833, age 19.

All of the grave stones of the Portuguese are inscribed at the base, "Erected by their Fellow Countrymen."

Francisco Joze Goncalues Labanja, stone # 126

Finally, at the south-east end of the Old Burying Ground are several fieldstones that may indicate where burials are. It is likely that some who couldn't afford to purchase a grave stone, marked the spot of their loved one's burial that way.

References : The Old Burying Ground's Segregated South-East End
Sleight, Harry D.. *Sag Harbor in Earlier Days*. Bridgehampton, NY : The Hampton Press, 1930.
Zaykowski, Dorothy Ingersoll. *Sag Harbor; the Story of an American*

Beauty. Mattituck, NY : Amereon, Ltd., 1991.
Census Records : Bridgehampton, NY
Sag Harbor Presbyterian Church Records
Oakland Cemetery list, John Jermain Library
Sag Harbor *Corrector,* January 1846.

D. Zaykowski

Nancy Maria Parker, stone # 164

SHORT BIO'S OF MISCELLANEOUS PEOPLE BURIED IN THE OLD BURYING GROUND

Shubal Coleman and family
(Gravestone # 27)

Shubal Coleman, born in 1771, was the son of Benjamin Coleman and his wife, Ruth. Benjamin came to Sag Harbor from Nantucket prior to 1776, and was engaged in shipping ventures. After the death of his wife and infant child in October and November 1801, Benjamin Coleman became a silversmith, and practiced that craft from 1802-1820. An advertisement he placed in *The Suffolk County Herald*, stated that he was looking for an apprentice to the gold and silversmith business. By 1820 Benjamin Coleman was doing blacksmith work as well.

The Coleman family lived in a house which stood on the site of the Municipal Building in Sag Harbor, and the 1776 census lists the Coleman's as having three males and two females in their family.

During the American Revolution, when many local families fled to Connecticut to escape the British occupation of Long Island, the Colemans stayed in Sag Harbor, and because Benjamin was a Quaker, he probably took no part in the war. An interesting story was related by Miss Anna Mulford in a paper read before the Sag Harbor Historical Society when she stated that during the Revolutionary War, a British soldier stationed in Sag Harbor gave Lucy Coleman his Bible for a loaf of bread. (Was Lucy Shubal's sister?)

Shubal Coleman died at the age of eighteen on July 3, 1789, and is buried in the Old Burying Ground. Perhaps his mother and the infant are buried there, too, in unmarked graves.

David Sherard
(Gravestone # 205)

David Sherard was said to have been the first native of Ireland to locate in Sag Harbor. He was first mentioned in 1800 when he was a twenty-one year old shipwright at the growing Port. It is possible that sickness was responsible for his untimely death, for David Sherard died on August 24, 1810, at the young age of thirty-one. He is buried in the Old Burying Ground.

William Lester Hall
(Gravestone # 208)

William Lester Hall died in Sag Harbor, where he had come on a visit to try to restore his health. Born in 1775 in Great Britain, William Lester Hall received his education in London and resided in the County of Effingham in the state of Georgia. (The Presbyterian Church records say South Carolina).

He worked as a cabinetmaker for the short time he was in Sag Harbor, but his frail health didn't improve and on August 4, 1803, at the age of twenty-eight years, he passed away. He is buried in the Old Burying Ground.

Samuel Solomon's Family
(Gravestones #135 and #136)

The Solomon's joined a growing number of African American residents in Sag Harbor which at that time included the Jacks, Birds, Brewsters and Tuckers.

Samuel Solomon was born in 1780, and on September 8, 1803 he married a woman named Mehetabel, who was born in 1782. Samuel and Mehetabel had at least two children, **Elizabeth (Eliza)** born in 1804, and a child who died at the age of one month, on December 15, 1814. Holly Solomon (date of birth unknown) may also have been a daughter of Samuel and Mehetabel.

Samuel joined the Sag Harbor Presbyterian Church in April of 1816, two months after the February 11th baptisms of Eliza and Holly. At that time, the present church had not yet been built, and the Solomon family would have attended "God's Old Barn" on the corner of Church and Sage Streets.

Eliza Solomon's short life ended on December 21, 1819, when she was but fifteen years old. Nine years later, her mother, Mehetabel died on June 25, 1828 at the age of forty-six. Samuel Solomon then married a second time to a woman known only as Hannah.

Eliza and Mehetabel are buried at the south end of the Old Burying Ground, their graves marked with stones #135 and #136. Samuel died in 1854 at the age of seventy-four. If Samuel and Hannah are interred there as well, they rest in unmarked graves.

Mehetabel Solomon, stone # 136

A Gans Solomon, born in 1795, and a member of the Bridgehampton Presbyterian Church, was possibly Samuel's brother. John Solomon, of Bridgehampton, who died November 2, 1828, may also have been a brother. John and a child of his who died November 17, 1838, are both listed in the Bridgehampton Presbyterian Church records, but it isn't known where they are buried.

The Gelston Family
(Gravestone's 259, 260, 264 and 265)

Hugh and Puah Gelston - (See Revolutionary War Patriots)

David Gelston was the nephew of Hugh Gelston, son of David

Gelston, Collector of the Port, and grandson of Deacon Maltby Gelston of Bridgehampton. He was born in 1775. His father, David, took an active part in the Revolutionary War and arranged for ships to carry refugees from Sag Harbor to Connecticut.

David Gelston was married briefly to Elizabeth Palmer before dying December 23, 1807 at the age of thirty-two. His widow, Elizabeth, lived to the age of seventy-seven, having died March 23, 1858. She never remarried and carried the grief of losing her husband at such an early age, for the rest of her life. Her epitaph tells it all. It reads: "For fifty years she tredded disconsolately in the path of widowhood, nor seemed ever to forget him to whom in early life she had wedded her earthly affections, but who in a seemingly untimely hour had been suddenly cut down a stroke of Providence that caused the throne of reason to tremble to its very center and despair and sorrow to usurp the place of trust and repose even to the end of her journey through life."

The Partridge Family
(Gravestones # 293, 294 and 295)

Asa Partridge, early resident of the village, was born in Preston, Connecticut in 1762. He came to Sag Harbor before 1790 and married Betsey Conklin. They were the parents on one son, Charles Henry Partridge, who was born in 1798.

In June 1791 Asa Partridge placed an advertisement in Frothingham's *Long Island Herald,* that stated he was opening a private school in Sag Harbor, where Arithmetic, Writing, English Grammar, Book Keeping and Elocution would be offered. After regular school hours, beginning at 4 pm, he would hold a "Ladies School" where morals and manners would be taught.

Asa Partridge was also the proprietor of a dry goods store and listed in the 1804-10 Business Directory. As a staunch Presbyterian, he had the distinction of being on a committee to receive proposals for building the 1817 church on the site of the Old Meeting House called, "God's Old Barn."

Charles Henry Partridge, who apparently was travelling out of the country, died at San Jose, Costa Rica on March 2, 1827, at the age of twenty-nine. Betsey Partridge died October 25, 1851 at the age of seventy-six, and Asa lived to the advanced age of ninety-two, having died December 10, 1854, in New York City. The Partridge family are all buried in the Old Burying Ground.

Marcy and Sally Crowell
(Gravestones # 3 and # 33)

Marcy Crowell and Sally Crowell were part of the extensive Crowell family that lived in Sag Harbor and North Haven, but the only two buried in the Old Burying Ground. Marcy, wife of Stephen Crowell was strangely enough born a Crowell, and probably somehow remotely related to Stephen. She was the daughter of Ebenezer and Mercy Gorham, and born February 14, 1769 in Massachusetts. Stephen and Marcy were the parents of nine children, all but their last two or three born in Massachusetts and Connecticut. Marcy died in Sag Harbor, along with her infant daughter, on December 5, 1793 and are buried in the Old Burying Ground, stone #33.

Sally Crowell, born in 1780, was the wife of Asa Crowell, son of Marcy and Stephen. Asa was a shoemaker in Sag Harbor and advertised his trade in the 1806 *Suffolk Gazette,* published in Sag Harbor. Sally died on October 10, 1806, at the age of twenty-six and is buried in the Old Burying Ground, stone #3. Asa later married Sophia Campbell of Connecticut. Other members of the Crowell family are interred in Oakland Cemetery.

Jonathan Hall and his sister Mary Hall
(Gravestones # 93 and # 94)

Jonathan and Mary Hall were the children of Reverend Daniel Hall and his wife, Lucretia. Reverend Hall came to Sag Harbor in 1797 and he became the first settled pastor of the Presbyterian Church. Along with Reverend Hall and his wife were their children, twenty-one year old Jonathan and eleven year old Mary. Jonathan Hall was a "book binder" and advertised in the local newspaper, *The Suffolk Gazette* from 1804-1810.
Mary Hall remained single all her life and died February 10, 1831 at the age of forty-five. Jonathan died at the age of sixty-one on

August 12, 1837. Both are buried in the Old Burying Ground.
Reverend Hall remained as pastor of the local church until the Spring
of 1806, when he was dismissed and he moved to Shelter Island, NY.
just north of Sag Harbor.

Some Tiny People in the Old Burying Ground

Mary Ann Coles and family
(Gravestone # 77)

Little **Mary Ann Coles**, daughter of Phebe and Thaddeus
Coles, only lived one year before her untimely death September 1,
1820. She was the third Coles child to die in the early 1800's, and the
only one whose grave in the Old Burying Ground is marked with a
stone. One sibling died at the age of two on September 7, 1827, and
the other died of scarlet fever on May 12, 1832, at the age of four. It is
likely they lie in unmarked graves in the Old Burying Ground, as
Oakland Cemetery had not yet opened.

In 1836 their daughter Fannie E. Coles was born. She was the
only Coles child to survive. As an adult, Fannie married Abram B.
Tunison, and became the mother of the noted Fannie Tunison, who
disabled from birth, learned to write, paint and do needlework by
holding the needle, pen and paintbrush with her tongue.
The Coles family and then the Tunison family lived on Hampton Street
in a tiny house three doors east of the junction of Division and
Hampton Streets. In 1774, Ichabod Coles, who may have been
Thaddeus Coles father, had a business at Sag Harbor's waterfront, and
it is believed the Coles house was moved from that location to its
Hampton Street site.

Thaddeus Coles died May 6, 1863 at the age of seventy-one
and Phebe March 12, 1873 at the age of 75. Their funerals were held
at the Sag Harbor Methodist-Episcopal Church and they were interred
in Oakland Cemetery.

Alden Spooner
(Gravestone # 58)

Little **Alden Spooner** lived but a brief two years, having been born in 1807 and having died November 28, 1809. His father, Alden Spooner, came to Sag Harbor as a young inexperienced printer at the age of twenty, and began publishing Sag Harbor's third newspaper, *The Suffolk Gazette*, on February 20, 1804. It was said that his entire fortune consisted of only a few dollars in his pocket, and scarcely a decent suit of clothes on his back. The paper was published until February 23, 1811.

Little Alden Jermain Spooner was baptised, along with his brother, Edward Bolton Spooner, on April 9, 1809. Seven months later two year old Alden was dead. He is the only Spooner buried in the Old Burying Ground, for two years later, his father and family moved to Brooklyn where he continued working in the newspaper business until his death.

John Hicks Overton and family
(Gravestone # 214)

John Hicks Overton was the son of James Overton and Jemima Fordham, who were married January 11, 1804, by Reverend Daniel Hall of the Presbyterian Church. Jemima died December 16, 1807, at the age of twenty-nine. An infant of James Overton and Jemima Fordham died February 10, 1807, ten months before Jemima. Another infant is buried with Jemima in the Old Burying Ground. James Overton was a "hatter" who advertised his business in the *Suffolk Gazette* from 1804-1811.

After the death of Jemima, James Overton married Elizabeth (who may have been Widow Elizabeth Hicks). John Hicks Overton, infant son of James and Elizabeth, died September 27, 1809, and is buried in the Old Burying Ground.

Henry Augustus Sleight and family
(Gravestone # 224)

Tiny **Henry Augustus Sleight** was born in 1828, the son of Henry Sleight and Cornelia Hildreth. His parents were married September 20, 1815, by Reverend John D. Gardiner of the Presbyterian Church.

Henry Augustus Sleight's father, Henry, upon leaving school, entered the newspaper office of Alden Spooner to learn the printing business. During the War of 1812, Henry Sleight served as a midshipman.

Two younger brothers, Luther Cornelius Sleight and an earlier Henry Augustus Sleight, were baptised on September 28, 1817 and September 23, 1820, respectively. The first Henry Augustus died September 23, 1820 at the age of fifteen months.

Henry Augustus Sleight (gravestone # 224) was undoubtedly named for his deceased brother, but his life was just as brief. He passed away at the age of one in September 1829. He is the only Sleight of that extensive Sag Harbor family who rests in the Old Burying Ground.

References : **Miscellaneous People Buried in the OBG**
Sleight, Harry D.. *Sag Harbor in Earlier Days*. Bridgehampton, NY : Hampton Press, 1930.
Sleight, Harry D.. *The Sleights of Sag Harbor*.
Hampton Press,
Zaykowski, Dorothy Ingersoll. *Sag Harbor, the Story of an American Beauty*. Mattituck, NY : Amereon Ltd., 1991.
Suffolk Gazette, miscellaneous issues 1804-1810.
OBG Inventories of William Wallace Tooker 1885, Louis Tooker Vail 1950, OBG Committee 2001.
Presbyterian Church records.

D. Zaykowski

ITHUEL HILL, STONE CUTTER

Ithuel Hill was Long Island's only 18th century documented stone cutter. His fine work can be seen in many of the old burial grounds of the north and south fork, as well as in Sag Harbor's Old Burying Ground. Hill descended from an old Connecticut family and came to Sag Harbor in 1789 following his marriage to Isabel Cornwall. Stone cutting went back three generations in the Hill family, and Ithuel learned the craft well, patterning his "soul effigies" after the Connecticut Valley style.

Along with his soul effigies, Ithuel Hill was known for his carvings of Masonic emblems, neo-classical designs, cherubs, and portrait stones. He usually carved his female likenesses full faced, while his male likenesses were done three-quarter view. The exquisite

Ithuel Hill,
STONE CUTTER, and ENGRAVER in STONE,

RESPECTFULLY informs the Public, that he carries on his Business in all its various branches at Sagg-Harbour, near the Landing, where he makes and Sells, Grave, Hearth, Grind, and all kinds of Building Stones, as Cheap as they can be purchased in America.

N.B. His Stone is brought from that noted quarry at Chatham, in Connecticut. They are very durable for Grave Stones, and stand the fire exceedingly well. Sagg-Harbour, July 5, 1791.

(Ithuel Hill's advertisement in *The Suffolk Gazette*, July 1802)

Benjamin Price, stone # 13
Stone shows curlicue mark, indicating Ithuel Hill's work

Hainulal Horton stone #223 in the Old Burying Ground is an example of Hill's fine workmanship. Ithuel Hill marked many of his stones with a downward spiraling curlicue under the inscription or epitaph, or a carved device resembling a curved symbol with a bulge at either end. A broken sunburst design was also used on occasion by Hill. The Sally Halsey stone #216 is another example of the carving done by Ithuel Hill.

Ithuel and Isabel Hill raised a large family while living in Sag Harbor. At least six children were born to them. They were of the Presbyterian faith and the church records list; John, baptized June 16, 1799, Sarah, baptized June 7, 1801, Louisa, baptised June 29, 1804, and Samuel, baptized April 6, 1809. Their other children were Mary, Julia and Edward, and most likely they were also baptized in the Presbyterian Church.

Ithuel Hill died in 1821 at Tauplin Cove, Massachusetts, while on a trip to regain his health. Isabel Hill and some of the Hill children are buried in Oakland Cemetery in Sag Harbor, while Ithuel was probably buried in Massachusetts.

Stone Types Used in the Old Burying Ground

Sandstone, slate, marble and schist are the types of stone monuments in the Old Burying Ground. Unlike many cemeteries on eastern Long Island, that removed their footstones to make maintenance easier, many footstones still remain in their original places at the Old Burying Ground. Support stones were also discovered while doing the inventory. Large rectangular pieces of sandstone or marble were buried against the front of the headstone to keep it from falling over. The tall Beebe gravestones along the east stone wall of the burying ground, were broken when the Presbyterian Church steeple fell on them during the 1938 hurricane. All having support stones, the headstones were unable to "give" in the rain-soaked ground, and either snapped off at the base or broke in several pieces.

Several fieldstones can be found in the Old Burying Ground, apparently marking the burial sites of those unable to afford to purchase a carved headstone. Wooden crosses may have been used as well, especially in the segregated section where much open space appears.

References : **Ithuel Hill, Stone Cutter**
Welch. Richard F.. Memento Mori; The Gravestones of Early Long Island 1680-1810. Syosset. New York : Friends for Long Island's Heritage. 1983.
Presbyterian Church Records

THE FENCE SURROUNDING THE OLD BURYING GROUND AT SAG HARBOR

There have been several fences enclosing the Old Burying Ground throughout the years. The original wooden fence constructed about the time the cemetery opened, was short lived. It was followed by a stone fence that was built in the early 1800's. This fence, collapsed sometime in the 1860's and was removed in 1863. It is reported that a substantial part of this stonewall was used to build the foundation of the Methodist Church on Madison Street. The next structure was a wood picket fence which, after a short seven years, succumbed to Mother Nature.

The last and current fence, was a wrought iron fence installed by the LVIS and completed in 1909 at a cost of $1000. Since World War II, the fence, like the cemetery itself, has suffered from much wear and tear. A number of the panels on the fence have been damaged by vandalism or vehicular accidents. Considerable rusting has occurred over the years although there has been some evidence of earlier repair and painting. When the Old Burying Ground Committee was first established in the late 1990's, rust was extensive, covering most of the fence. The cost of replacing this fence with a similar structure was considered. But estimates of the cost were prohibitive.

A few members of the committee wire brushed two panels to determine the extent of the rust damage and were pleased to find that rust was primarily on the surface. Over the next four years, with the help of various people, we were able to wire brush the whole fence on Latham and Madison Street sides. Following that, we have just completed applying a primer and finished coat of paint to the entire fence. Hopefully the result of this long and tedious job will hold up well for many years to come.

References : **The Fence Surrounding the Old Burying Ground**
Zaykowski. Dorothy Ingersoll. *Sag Harbor; the Story of an American Beauty*. Mattituck : Amereon. Ltd.. 1991.
LVIS History. Clippings. John Jermain Library. Sag Harbor.
P. Saurer

John Goodwin, Jr., stone # 206
(The only "schist" stone in the OBG)

The iron fence on the Madison Street side

THE EMBANKMENT

Erosion of the Old Burying Ground embankment on Madison Street between Latham and Union Streets is as much of a problem now as it was in 1860 when the decision was made to remove 139 graves to the new Oakland Cemetery. After the widening of Madison Street, it made the stone wall holding up the steep rise unstable. About eight years ago the Southampton Town mowers removed the native roses and day lilies that had helped to hold soil in place among the oak and maple tree roots. Now there are rivers of mud on the sidewalk after every storm and thaw, and we have gotten much advice about what to do.

The landscapers we have consulted recommend native grasses and plants like the ones that were uprooted. Kevin McAllister, the Peconic Baykeeper, was interested in making the bank a project to demonstrate the benign runoff from native plantings which need no fertilizer or pesticides, but even these plants are expensive to buy and get started and as yet the money is on no one's budget. One alternative is to plant the groundcover Myrtle (periwinkle), and soon we might have an appeal for these plants that have become too rampant in local gardens. But in these drought times we are also thinking of a row of rocks or cobblestone inside the newly painted fence as a partial solution.

The oaks along the bank are good trees, and they and the maples need pruning to let in light which might allow native plants to appear spontaneously. This would be an attractive and historically appropriate solution.

S. Rowland

FACTS OF INTEREST

1. Of the three hundred and thirty-five burials in the Old Burying Ground, seventy-two are children under the age of three, nine between the ages of four and ten, and twenty-two between the ages of eleven and twenty. Almost one third are twenty years old and younger.

2. It is said that the first two burials in the Old Burying Ground were the 1767 burials of the infant children of Sag Harbor Tory Innkeeper, James Howell. Tradition says that the children's mother wept because they were "so far off in the woods." Most of the village of Sag Harbor was north of Union Street at that time. (There are no gravestones marking where these burials are).

3. Nathaniel Baker and John Peirson (stone #47) lost their lives on February 25, 1815 while celebrating the return of peace between the United States and Great Britain.

4. Sarah Fordham and her husband, Nathan Fordham (stone #244) died November 12, 1805, within eleven hours of each other and are buried in the same grave.

5. William Havens (stone #198) drowned off Cape Cod, Massachusetts, November 21, 1798, while piloting the Brig, *Lucy*. He was captain of the privateers, *Beaver*, *Jay* and *Retaliation* during the Revolutionary War.

6. One hundred thirty-nine graves were removed from the Madison Street side of the Old Burying Ground in 1860 and re-interred in Oakland Cemetery. The reason; the possibility of spring rains exposing the remains when the road was widened.

7. Charles Henry Partridge (stone #293) reads that he died in Costa Rica, in San Jose, formerly the Kingdom of Central America, on March 22, 1827.

8. Field stones in the southern part of the Old Burying Ground may mark burial sites.

9. A Portuguese sailor, Manuel Francisco (stone #129) lost his life

when he fell from the foremast of the whaleship, *Hannibal,* on June 24, 1833.

10. Nathaniel Mott's (stone #334) was discovered buried face down next to the wall in the Old Burying Ground on April 22, 2001. It was found one hundred seventy-six years to the day that Nathanial died, April 22, 1825. One year old Nathaniel is not on any previous inventory list.

11. Ithuel Hill, was the only documented18th century stonecutter on Long Island when he came to Sag Harbor in 1789.

12. Frederic Fordham, sixteen, was confined to a Wallabout Bay Prison Ship during the Revolutionary War and died shortly after being released, due to the treatment he received while imprisoned.

HELPFUL HINTS
"Reducing Power Mower Damage"

Power mowers and weed-whackers can be formidable culprits when it comes to harming gravestones. If you've noticed a straight horizontal scratch along the base of a stone, or a chip or two flaked off the edge of the stone, it may well be the work of grass-cutting machines.

What to do? Other than hand-clipping around each stone, there are a couple of suggestions you might take into consideration. If your burying ground is small in size, you may try removing the grass that is against the stone and leave a rectangular area of dirt. Some recommend filling in a space around the base of the stone with pebbles or wood chips.

Maybe you can come up with a more ingenius and less intrusive looking method, but in a large burying ground with many stones, the easiest and safest way is to take care when cutting the grass. It may take a little longer, but the results will be far less damaging.

Josiah Hand, stone # 85
(Revolutionary War Patriot)

Segregated South-end of OBG

Mary Duvall, stone # 176

Emmeline Latham, stone # 57

Index of Names

ABOUT THE AUTHOR

Dorothy Ingersoll Zaykowski is a fourth generation Sag Harborite with long interest in local history. She is the author of, *Sag Harbor: The Story of an American Beauty*, a 394-page book published in 1991 on the founding and growth of the whaling port of Sag Harbor, and many articles of local history published in the *Sag Harbor Express*. Ms. Zaykowski was Curator of Local History at the John Jermain Memorial Library in Sag Harbor, Museum Administrator at the Bridgehampton Historical Society, Bridgehampton, LI, NY, Trustee and Office Manager at the Sag Harbor Historical Society and member of the Old Burying Ground Committee.

This informative book was compiled with contributions from Committee members, Andrea Meyer, Susan Rowland, Barbara Schwartz and Paul Saurer. At present Dorothy Ingersoll Zaykowski is co-authoring a book on the history of North Haven, Long Island.

www.ingramcontent.com/pod-product-compliance
Lightning Source LLC
Chambersburg PA
CBHW052038270326
41931CB00012B/2537